CORE SKILLS

ISBN-13: 978-1-4190-3410-7
ISBN-10:   1-4190-3410-3

The paper used in this book comes from sustainable resources.

Printed in the United States of America.
1 2 3 4 5 6 7 8 9   862   10 09 08 07 06

Steck Vaughn™

A Harcourt Achieve Imprint

www.HarcourtSchoolSupply.com
1-800-531-5015

Contents

Contents
Core Skills Spelling 6, SV 9781419034107

Introduction

Core Skills: Spelling is a research-based, systematic spelling program developed to help students master spelling. The program is based on three critical goals for students:

- to learn to spell common spelling patterns and troublesome words
- to learn strategies related to sounds and spelling patterns
- to link spelling and meaning

Each book in the *Core Skills: Spelling* program is composed of 30 skill lessons. The majority of skill lessons in this program focus on spellings of vowel sounds. Other skill lessons focus on word structure and content-area words.

Key features of this book include:

- study steps that focus learning,
- a spelling table that contains common spellings for consonant and vowel sounds,
- lessons that build competency and provide visual reinforcement,
- word study that expands vocabulary and meaning,
- engaging vocabulary and context activities that encourage students to explore word meanings and use words in meaningful contexts, and
- challenge sections that present opportunities to enrich vocabulary and extend spelling skills.

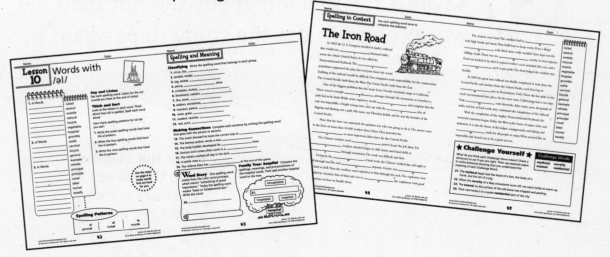

Study Steps to Learn a Word

 Say the word. What consonant sounds do you hear? What vowel sounds do you hear? How many syllables do you hear?

 Look at the letters in the word. Think about how each sound is spelled. Find any spelling patterns or parts that you know. Close your eyes. Picture the word in your mind.

 Spell the word aloud.

 Write the word. Say each letter as you write it.

 Check the spelling. If you did not spell the word correctly, use the study steps again.

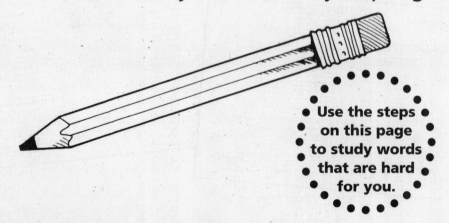

Use the steps on this page to study words that are hard for you.

Study Steps to Learn a Word
Core Skills Spelling 6, SV 9781419034107

Spelling Table

Sound	Spellings	Examples	Sound	Spellings	Examples
/ă/	a ai au	catalog, plaid, laughed	/ō/	o o_e oa oe ou ough ow eau ew	noble, throne, loan, toe, poultry, although, grown, plateau, sew
/ā/	a a_e ai aigh ay ea eigh ey	agent, invade, stain, straight, mayor, break, weighted, surveyor	/oi/	oi oy	coin, enjoyable
/ä/	a ea ua	salami, heart, guard	/ô/	a au augh aw o oa ou ough	chalk, laundry, daughter, awful, often, coarse, course, thought
/âr/	are air ere eir	aware, dairy, there, their	/o͝o/	oo o ou u	book, wolf, could, education
/b/	b bb	barber, cabbage	/o͞o/	oo eu ew u u_e ue o o_e oe ou ui	smooth, neutral, threw, truth, refuse, clue, whom, improve, canoe, coupon, juice
/ch/	ch tch t	sandwich, kitchen, amateur			
/d/	d dd	dawn, meddle			
/ĕ/	e ea a ai ay ie ue	length, instead, many, against, says, friend, guest	/ou/	ou ow	couch, howl
/ē/	e e_e ea ee ei eo ey i i_e ie y	meter, scene, speaker, degrees, receive, people, monkey, piano, gasoline, brief, memory	/p/	p pp	pass, apply
			/r/	r rh rr wr	ring, rhythm, worry, wrong
			/s/	s sc ss c	slant, scene, dress, justice
/f/	f ff gh ph	fever, different, laugh, graph	/sh/	sh s ce ci	flashlight, sugar, ocean, special
/g/	g gg	glue, struggle	/shən/	tion	station
/h/	h wh	half, whole	/t/	t tt ed	tennis, attention, thanked
/ĭ/	a a_e e ee ei i u ui y	spinach, luggage, select, been, forfeit, million, business, build, myth	/th/	th	whether
			/th/	th	throw
/ī/	i i_e ie igh uy y y_e eye	science, strike, die, sigh, buy, deny, style, eye	/ŭ/	u o oe oo ou	result, among, does, flood, touch
/îr/	er ear eer eir ere yr	periodical, hear, cheer, weird, here, lyrics	/ûr/	ear er ere ir or our ur	earn, personal, were, thirsty, worst, flourish, curly
/j/	j g dg	justice, voyages, pledge	/v/	v f	violin, of
/k/	k c cc ck ch	kitchen, cabinet, soccer, clockwise, choir	/w/	w wh o	wind, wharf, once
			/y/	y	yolk
/ks/	x	excavation	/yo͞o/	eau eu u u_e	beautiful, feud, human, use
/kw/	qu	quiet	/z/	z zz s ss x	zone, quizzical, wise, dessert, xylophone
/l/	l ll	label, umbrella			
/m/	m mb mm mn	meter, thumb, mammal, condemn	/zh/	s	treasure
/n/	n kn nn	novel, knife, tunnel	/ə/	a e i o u ai ou	hospital, weaken, principle, person, circus, captain, various
/ng/	n ng	thank, strengthen			
/ŏ/	o ow a	ecology, knowledge, equality			

www.harcourtschoolsupply.com

Spelling Table
Core Skills Spelling 6, SV 9781419034107

Lesson 1

Words with /ă/

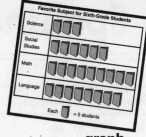

graph

1. a Words

_____
_____
_____
_____
_____
_____
_____
_____
_____
_____
_____
_____
_____
_____
_____
_____
_____
_____
_____

2. au Word

_____

salmon
attract
catalog
mammal
camera
balance
rapid
laughed
magnet
gravity
command
alphabet
graph
passed
accent
scramble
imagine
sandwich
paragraph
photograph

Say and Listen

Say each spelling word. Listen for the /ă/ sound you hear in *salmon*.

Think and Sort

Some of the spelling words have more than one *a*, but only one has the /ă/ sound. Look at the letters in each word. Think about how /ă/ is spelled. Spell each word aloud.

How many spelling patterns for /ă/ do you see?

1. Write the nineteen spelling words that have the *a* pattern. Underline each *a* that has the /ă/ sound.

2. Write the one spelling word that has the *au* pattern.

Use the steps on page 4 to study words that are hard for you.

Spelling Patterns

a	au
c**a**talog	l**au**ghed

Spelling and Meaning

Clues Write the spelling word for each clue.

1. what a tightrope walker needs   _____
2. why we don't fall off the earth   _____
3. a list of available items   _____
4. what a photographer uses   _____
5. what iron is attracted to   _____
6. what a mathematician might draw   _____
7. what the Earl of Sandwich ate   _____
8. a section of writing   _____
9. a mark found in a dictionary   _____
10. what a chinook and a sockeye are   _____
11. what a bear is   _____

Synonyms Synonyms are words that have the same or almost the same meaning. Write the spelling word that is a synonym for the underlined word.

12. A parade of five hundred soldiers <u>went</u> by the courthouse.   _____
13. The general will <u>direct</u> the entire army.   _____
14. The flowers in my grandfather's yard <u>draw</u> bees.   _____
15. We had to <u>hurry</u> to make it to the train station on time.   _____
16. Victor took a <u>snapshot</u> of Ashley.   _____
17. The speedboat raced along at a <u>fast</u> rate.   _____
18. The audience <u>chuckled</u> at the comic's jokes.   _____
19. Can you <u>picture</u> what life in space would be like?   _____

Word Story One spelling word comes from the first two letters of the Greek alphabet, *alpha* and *beta*. *Alphabetos* became the name for all of the Greek letters. Write the spelling word that comes from *alphabetos*.

20. _____

Family Tree: *photograph* Compare the spellings, meanings, and pronunciations of the *photograph* words. Then add another *photograph* word to the tree.

photographed

21.

photography   photographer

photograph

Lesson 1: Words with /ă/
Core Skills Spelling 6, SV 9781419034107

Name: _____   Date: _____

Spelling in Context

Use each spelling word once to complete the story.

Snake River Snapshots

by Derrick Williams

My sister, Shauna Williams, a budding photographer, and I took a day trip down the Snake River in Washington. Shauna's job was to _____ interesting animals. My job
1
was to report the experience in one exciting, well-written _____ after another.
2

Getting There

Our journey began in Lewistown, Idaho. Mom, Dad, Shauna, and I held our breath as the plane made a steep and _____ descent into the airport. Once on the ground,
3
we had to quickly grab our things and _____ down the steps of the small plane
4
to meet our guide. Shauna carried her _____, extra lenses, and lots of film. She
5
was planning to try out some new supplies she had ordered from a photography
_____. One of them was a new zoom lens. She wanted close-up pictures of
6
_____ and other fish leaping out of the water in the river.
7

Packing for the Trip

Mom handed us our jackets. Dad had brought food—a peanut butter
_____ for each of us and tons of juice. I had my laptop computer. The guide
8
reminded us to travel as light as possible. "You'll be sorry if you have a heavy backpack," he said.
"The laws of _____ will catch up with you, and you'll end up with a sore
9
back."

I left my laptop on land with my parents, but I did take my compass. Shauna reminded me
not to get the compass close to her camera. Photographers think the _____ in
10
a compass can spoil their film.

On Our Way

Jack, our capable rafting guide, spoke with a lilting Canadian

_____. He _____ good-naturedly and
            11   12

helped Shauna keep her _____ as she juggled her camera
                                  13

equipment to get into the raft.

We tried not to _____ any attention from the animals
                          14

as we floated quietly down the river. Shauna wanted to shoot pictures of fish

as well as deer, bear, and any other _____ that might appear
                                              15

along the riverbank. As soon as we got in the raft, she began to snap photos. I

asked her to tell how she planned her shots. "I pretend that the scene is a

circle _____, and I divide what I see into sections," she said.
              16

"Then I _____ where an animal is hiding and stay
                17

prepared. Sooner or later, an animal appears."

The Photo Finish

As we floated along, we _____ an antelope, a bear, and
                                  18

coho salmon. We seemed to find an animal for each letter in the

_____. Shauna commented that some of the animals
        19

looked as if they were posing on _____. When I saw the
                                            20

deer and salmon photographs later, I had to agree.

★ Challenge Yourself ★

Challenge Words

immaculate
pamphlet
flabbergasted
sassafras

What do you think each Challenge Word means? Check a dictionary to see if you are right. Then use separate paper to write sentences showing that you understand the meaning of each Challenge Word.

21. You won't find a speck of dirt in an **immaculate** kitchen.

22. I picked up an interesting **pamphlet** at the health fair.

23. I was **flabbergasted** when the waiter told us our lunch was free.

24. My grandmother can make tea from the bark of **sassafras** roots.

Lesson 2
Words with /ā/

entertain

Say and Listen
Say each spelling word. Listen for the /ā/ sound you hear in *trace*.

Think and Sort
Look at the letters in each word. Think about how /ā/ is spelled. Spell each word aloud.

How many spelling patterns for /ā/ do you see?

1. Write the one spelling word that has the *a* pattern.

2. Write the eight spelling words that have the *a-consonant-e* pattern. Underline the *a-consonant-e* pattern in each word.

3. Write the two spelling words that have the *ay* or *ey* pattern.

4. Write the six spelling words that have the *ai* pattern.

5. Write the three spelling words that have the *aigh* or *eigh* pattern.

Use the steps on page 4 to study words that are hard for you.

1. *a* Word

_____

2. *a-consonant-e* Words

_____
_____
_____
_____
_____
_____
_____
_____

3. *ay, ey* Words

_____
_____

4. *ai* Words

_____
_____
_____
_____
_____
_____

5. *aigh, eigh* Words

_____
_____
_____

trace
mayor
parade
escape
invade
complain
misplace
stain
raincoat
remain
safety
neighborhood
entertain
hesitate
explain
agent
congratulate
straight
weighted
disobey

Spelling Patterns

a	a-consonant-e		ay
agent	tr**a**c**e**		m**ay**or
ey	**ai**	**aigh**	**eigh**
disob**ey**	st**ai**n	str**aigh**t	w**eigh**ted

Name: Date:

Spelling and Meaning

Antonyms   Antonyms are words that have opposite meanings. Write the spelling word that is an antonym of each word.

1. danger   _____
2. retreat   _____
3. obey   _____
4. crooked   _____
5. find   _____
6. bore   _____
7. leave   _____

Definitions   Write the spelling word for each definition. Use a dictionary if you need to.

8. to pause before acting   _____
9. loaded down   _____
10. to discolor, spot, or soil   _____
11. to get away or get free   _____
12. to say something is wrong or annoying   _____
13. an area within a larger town or city   _____
14. a waterproof coat worn for protection from rain   _____
15. the highest official in city or town government   _____
16. to make plain or clear   _____
17. a small quantity or amount   _____
18. to praise someone for success or achievement   _____
19. to pass by in a large group   _____

Word Story   The Latin word *agere* meant "to do or act." From it comes one of the spelling words. The word means "someone who acts on behalf of someone else." Write the word.

20. _____

Family Tree: *explain*   Compare the spellings, meanings, and pronunciations of the *explain* words. Then add another *explain* word to the tree.

unexplainable

21.

explaining   explained

explain

www.harcourtschoolsupply.com
© Harcourt Achieve Inc. All rights reserved.

11

Lesson 2: Words with /ā/
Core Skills Spelling 6, SV 9781419034107

Spelling in Context

Use each spelling word once to complete the story.

Solving the Missing Watch Case

It was Thanksgiving, and Will and Claudia had ridden their bikes

into town to see the Thanksgiving _____. "My friend
                                          1

Nathan Robinson lives in that house over there," Claudia said. "His father

is the new _____ of Leesboro. Let's stop by and say
                    2

hello." Claudia put out her hand to signal a left turn. She'd just taken a

course in bicycle _____ and didn't want to
                          3

_____ the traffic rules.
        4

Nathan answered the doorbell. "Hi, Nathan," Claudia said. "We were

just in the _____. This is Will Miranda."
                    5

"Hi," Nathan said. "Come on in. I need help. I've been looking for my gold pocket watch. It's

gone and I can't _____ why it's missing. It's a really old one, too, with an
                          6

outdoor scene etched on the cover. How could I _____ something like that?"
                                                          7

"Don't worry," Claudia replied as she tightened the belt on her _____.
                                                                          8

"We'll help you find it."

Nathan didn't _____ for a moment. He led them _____
                      9   10

to the table where he'd left the watch. "Something weird is going on around here. Everyone is in a

different room, and no one will let me in. And now the watch is missing."

"Who is in the house?" Will asked in the serious tone of an FBI _____. "If
                                                                          11

everyone who's here will _____ in the same place, I think we'll be able to
                                  12

_____ your watch."
        13

"Well," replied Nathan. "My sister, Emma, is baking. Uncle Sol said he was going upstairs to

take a shower. My father is locked up in the basement and left definite instructions not to

_____ his privacy. And my brother, 'Randall the Great
      14
Magician,' said he was busy getting ready to _____ us in
                                                    15
the den with some daring new _____ act."
                                      16

   Just then, Mr. Robinson walked into the room. He was

_____ down with a large painting, and there was a green
      17
paint _____ on his apron. "Happy birthday, son," he said,
          18
handing Nathan the painting and the gold watch.

   "Wow!" exclaimed Nathan. "That explains it. You painted the scene from
my watch. It's great, Dad. Thanks a million!"

   Suddenly people burst in from everywhere. Emma carried a birthday
cake. Uncle Sol was hidden by balloons. Randall came in and began to

_____ about all the noise when a present popped out of his
      19
hat!

   Nathan turned to Will and Claudia. "I guess you're just in time for a
party!" he said. "By the way, I want to _____ you on your
                                               20
fine detective work!"

   "Oh, it was nothing," Will said.

   "Happy Birthday, Nathan!" Claudia exclaimed. "Another mystery is
solved!"

| trace |
| mayor |
| parade |
| escape |
| invade |
| complain |
| misplace |
| stain |
| raincoat |
| remain |
| safety |
| neighborhood |
| entertain |
| hesitate |
| explain |
| agent |
| congratulate |
| straight |
| weighted |
| disobey |

★ Challenge Yourself ★

Challenge Words

implication
ascertain
incorporate
disdain

Use a dictionary to answer these questions. Then use
separate paper to write sentences showing that you
understand the meaning of each Challenge Word.

21. Does a smile give the **implication** that you are happy?

_____

22. Can a group report **incorporate** the ideas of each member? _____

23. Would most people in trouble **disdain** an offer of help? _____

24. Should you **ascertain** that a rumor is true before you believe it? _____

Lesson 3

Words with /ĕ/

tennis

1. e Words

_____
_____
_____
_____
_____
_____
_____
_____
_____
_____
_____

2. ea Words

_____
_____
_____
_____
_____
_____

3. ue Words

_____
_____

4. ai Word

_____

length
tennis
instead
guessed
envelope
pleasant
energy
headache
echo
excellent
breakfast
insects
guest
measure
restaurant
against
treasure
metric
separate
success

Say and Listen

Say each spelling word. Listen for the /ĕ/ sound you hear in *length*.

Think and Sort

Some of the spelling words have more than one e, but only one has the /ĕ/ sound. Look at the letters in each word. Think about how /ĕ/ is spelled. Spell each word aloud.

How many spelling patterns for /ĕ/ do you see?

1. Write the eleven spelling words that have the e pattern. Underline each e that has the /ĕ/ sound.

2. Write the six spelling words that have the *ea* pattern.

3. Write the two spelling words that have the *ue* pattern.

4. Write the one spelling word that has the *ai* pattern.

Use the steps
on page 4 to
study words
that are hard
for you.

Spelling Patterns

e	ea	ue	ai
le**ng**th	inst**ea**d	g**ue**st	ag**ai**nst

Name: _____   Date: _____

Spelling and Meaning

Classifying Write the spelling word that belongs in each group.

1. snails, worms, _____
2. volleyball, soccer, _____
3. width, height, _____
4. stomachache, earache, _____
5. company, visitor, _____
6. stamp, letter, _____
7. dinner, lunch, _____
8. great, wonderful, _____
9. riches, wealth, _____
10. supposed, suspected, _____
11. divide, set apart, _____
12. in place of, rather than, _____

Clues Write the spelling word for each clue.

13. This is the opposite of *for*.   _____
14. This word describes a warm, calm day.   _____
15. Solar power and electricity are types of this.   _____
16. If you hear a repeated sound, it might be this.   _____
17. This word names a system of measurement.   _____
18. People use rulers and yardsticks to do this.   _____
19. This is the opposite of *failure*.   _____

Word Story One spelling word comes from the Old French word *restorer*, which meant "to restore or refresh." The spelling word names a place where people go to restore their hungry bodies. Write the word.

20. _____

Family Tree: *separate* Compare the spellings, meanings, and pronunciations of the *separate* words. Then add another *separate* word to the tree.

inseparable

21.

separated   separately

separate

Spelling in Context

Use each spelling word once to complete the story.

The Contest

One morning a message arrived in Sherwood Forest. Robin Hood had just finished

eating his _____ 1 when he opened the letter, which had been tucked into a

beautiful _____ 2 . "I wish you a _____ 3 morning," wrote

the queen. "I bid you to be my _____ 4 this day at the king's

archery tournament and to compete _____ 5 the king's

archers."

In those days a contest with bows and arrows was as popular as the later

game of _____ 6 . People flocked to an archery tournament from all parts of

the kingdom. While they prepared to watch the contest, they dined on small cakes and cider

that they bought not at a fine _____ 7 but from a vendor on the street.

Who would win the _____ 8 offered by the king? The king naturally

favored his own archers, Clifton, Tepus, and Gilbert, and wished them much

_____ 9 . When he saw the queen's archers, led by Robin Hood, he

_____ 10 that the queen was up to mischief.

"These rascals are no match for my archers," the king growled to the queen. "They crawl

out of the forest like so many small _____ 11 ."

"Your majesty," said the queen, "if my archers should win _____ 12 of

yours, I ask only that you be fair with your treasure."

Trusting that each of his _____ 13 archers would win, the king accepted.

"Let the game begin!" he roared. The crowd repeated the king's command in a booming

_____ 14 that traveled the _____ 15 of the field. Everyone

turned to watch.

First Clifton was paired against one of Robin's men. Each marksman used his skill and

_____ 16 to shoot the arrows, and each arrow hit the target. The distance

between each arrow was so short that the best _____ of it
                                                                    17

would have been the millimeter of the _____ system.
                                                            18

    Then Tepus shot against Little John. Again the archers were evenly

matched. Finally Gilbert, the King's finest archer, shot against Robin. The

target was a thin willow wand in the ground. "I can hardly see it," said Gilbert.

He closed his eyes as if annoyed by a painful _____. His
                                                                  19

arrow whizzed by the willow, but Robin's arrow split the willow into two

_____ pieces.
        20

    And so it was that Robin and his merry men enjoyed the king's treasure.

<table>
<tr><td>length</td></tr>
<tr><td>tennis</td></tr>
<tr><td>instead</td></tr>
<tr><td>guessed</td></tr>
<tr><td>envelope</td></tr>
<tr><td>pleasant</td></tr>
<tr><td>energy</td></tr>
<tr><td>headache</td></tr>
<tr><td>echo</td></tr>
<tr><td>excellent</td></tr>
<tr><td>breakfast</td></tr>
<tr><td>insects</td></tr>
<tr><td>guest</td></tr>
<tr><td>measure</td></tr>
<tr><td>restaurant</td></tr>
<tr><td>against</td></tr>
<tr><td>treasure</td></tr>
<tr><td>metric</td></tr>
<tr><td>separate</td></tr>
<tr><td>success</td></tr>
</table>

★ Challenge Yourself ★

Challenge Words

imperative
indelible
repel
questionnaire

Write the Challenge Word for each clue. Check a dictionary to see if you are right. Then use separate paper to write sentences showing that you understand the meaning of each Challenge Word.

21. This kind of ink is permanent. _____

22. You may fill out one of these to take part in a survey. _____

23. This kind of task must be done. _____

24. Insect spray will do this to mosquitoes and flies. _____

Name: _____ Date: _____

Lesson 4
Words with /ə/

lemonade

1. e Words
_____
_____
_____
_____
_____
_____
_____
_____
_____
_____

2. o Words
_____
_____
_____
_____
_____
_____
_____
_____

3. ai Words
_____
_____

darken
person
weaken
often
lessen
onion
listen
quicken
prison
strengthen
lemonade
seldom
lesson
fasten
kitchen
ransom
captain
mountains
soften
custom

Say and Listen
Say each spelling word. Listen for the vowel sound in the syllable that is not stressed.

Think and Sort
The weak vowel sound that you hear in unstressed syllables is called a **schwa**. It is shown as /ə/. Look at the letters in each word. Think about how /ə/ is spelled. Spell each word aloud.

How many spelling patterns for /ə/ do you see?

1. Write the ten spelling words that have /ə/ spelled e.

2. Write the eight spelling words that have /ə/ spelled o.

3. Write the two spelling words that have /ə/ spelled *ai*.

pleasant
among
company
confront

sentence
problem
enemy

Use the steps on page 4 to study words that are hard for you.

Spelling Patterns

e	o	ai
fast**e**n	less**o**n	capt**ai**n

Lesson 4: Words with /ə/
Core Skills Spelling 6, SV 9781419034107

Spelling and Meaning

Antonyms Write the spelling word that is an antonym of each word.

1. valleys _____
2. harden _____
3. lighten _____
4. strengthen _____
5. rarely _____
6. frequently _____
7. increase _____
8. unfasten _____

Analogies An analogy states that two words go together in the same way as two others. Write the spelling word that completes each analogy.

9. *Eye* is to *see* as *ear* is to _____.

10. *Energize* is to _____ as *construct* is to *build*.

11. *Sleeping* is to *bedroom* as *cooking* is to _____.

12. *Kidnapper* is to _____ as *burglar* is to *jewelry*.

13. *Clinic* is to *hospital* as *jail* is to _____.

14. *Learn* is to _____ as *draw* is to *picture*.

15. *Lettuce* is to *cabbage* as _____ is to *garlic*.

16. *Men* is to *man* as *people* is to _____.

17. *Practice* is to _____ as *rule* is to *law*.

18. *Lemon* is to _____ as *egg* is to *omelet*.

19. *Length* is to *lengthen* as *quick* is to _____.

Word Story From the Latin word *caput*, which meant "head," came the Old French word *capitaine*, which meant "chief." One of the spelling words comes from *capitaine*. Write the word.

20. _____

Family Tree: *person* Compare the spellings, meanings, and pronunciations of the *person* words. Then add another *person* word to the tree.

personification

21. _____

impersonal   personal

person

Spelling in Context

Use each spelling word once to complete the selection.

Special Agent for the FBI

The police _____ hands the
1

_____ note to a special agent. The agent handles it
2

carefully. It may contain fingerprints. Other agents are already searching

the room for evidence that will help them find the kidnapper and

rescue the kidnapped _____. The special agents are
3

from the Federal Bureau of Investigation, or FBI. Since 1908, FBI agents

have solved crimes such as kidnapping, bank robberies, and spying.

How does an ordinary person become a special agent? The FBI has a special training

academy. It lies 50 miles south of FBI headquarters in Washington, D.C., and 100 miles east

of the line of _____ called the Appalachians.
4

The FBI Training Academy is _____ seen by outsiders. It has a
5

library and places for research. It also has a _____ that provides meals for
6

trainees. Then there is Hogan's Alley, a mock city that imitates life in a real city. Training

lasts 16 weeks, and trainees receive more than 600 hours of instruction. They are

_____ found in special training classes.
7

As has been the _____ for many years, trainees spend hours
8

exercising and learning self-defense. The training is meant to _____ the
9

body and _____ the mind. Trainees also learn such skills as how to
10

quickly _____ handcuffs around a suspect's wrists.
11

Trainees learn about science, too. They learn about different kinds of scientific tests.

Special tests performed after death can tell FBI agents how a person died. One test can

even reveal that a person drank a glass of _____ or ate a
            12
cheeseburger with _____.
                    13

　　Trainees go to classes to learn about modern communications and

computers. One _____ they learn is how to use a wiretap
                 14

to secretly _____ to people's conversations.
             15

　　Trainees also learn how to interview suspects. They learn that some

suspects relax if the lights are turned down to _____ the
                                                  16
room. Trainees also learn when to raise their voice and when to

_____ it to almost a whisper to ask a suspect questions.
   17

Good interviewing skills _____ the chances of an innocent
                          18

person being charged with a crime.

　　Trainees take a final test in Hogan's Alley. They use everything they have

learned to solve a crime. Even a tough suspect may _____
                                                     19

and confess in the face of strong evidence. Thanks to excellent training, FBI

agents make sure that guilty persons go to _____.
                                             20

| darken |
| person |
| weaken |
| often |
| lessen |
| onion |
| listen |
| quicken |
| prison |
| strengthen |
| lemonade |
| seldom |
| lesson |
| fasten |
| kitchen |
| ransom |
| captain |
| mountains |
| soften |
| custom |

★ Challenge Yourself ★

Challenge Words

tranquil
disconnect
fusion
lateral

Use a dictionary to answer these questions. Then use
separate paper to write sentences showing that you
understand the meaning of each Challenge Word.

21. Would a lake be **tranquil** during a storm?

_____

22. Will a lamp work if you **disconnect** it from the wall outlet? _____

23. Does heat make the **fusion** of two metals possible? _____

24. Would it be smart for someone at the top of a ladder to make a **lateral** move?

_____

Lesson 5
Geography Words

North America

Say and Listen
Say the spelling words. Listen for the number of syllables in each word.

Think and Sort
All of the spelling words name places around the world. Some of the place names, such as North America, contain two words.

1. Write the thirteen two-word place names.

2. A syllable is a word part or word with one vowel sound. Sort the remaining seven spelling words by number of syllables and write them under the headings at left.

1. Two-Word Names

_____
_____
_____
_____
_____
_____
_____
_____
_____
_____
_____
_____
_____

2. One-Syllable Name

_____

Two-Syllable Names

_____
_____
_____

Three-Syllable Names

_____
_____

Four-Syllable Names

_____

Caribbean Sea
Himalayas
North America
Indian Ocean
Australia
Atlantic Ocean
Asia
Pacific Ocean
Alps
Nile River
Africa
Rocky
    Mountains
Central America
Mediterranean
    Sea
Appalachian
    Mountains
Andes
Europe
Mississippi River
South America
Amazon River

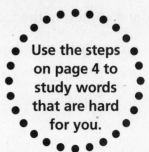

Use the steps on page 4 to study words that are hard for you.

Spelling Patterns

One Syllable	Two Syllables
Alps	**An•d**es

Three Syllables	Four Syllables
Af•ri•ca	**Him•a•la•**yas

Name: _____ Date: _____

Spelling and Meaning

What's the Answer? Write the spelling word that answers each question.

1. What mountain range is found in south-central Europe? _____
2. What is the longest river in Africa? _____
3. What body of water is found in the central United States? _____
4. What continent extends from the Atlantic Ocean to Asia? _____

Clues Write the spelling word for each clue.

5. chief mountain range in North America _____
6. mountains in South America _____
7. highest mountains in the world _____
8. ocean between Africa and Australia _____
9. area between Mexico and South America _____
10. body of water that is part of the Atlantic Ocean _____
11. sea between Africa and Europe _____
12. largest continent _____
13. longest river in South America _____
14. continent southeast of North America _____
15. continent between Atlantic and Indian oceans _____
16. mountains found in eastern North America _____
17. continent on which Canada is located _____
18. continent between Indian and Pacific oceans _____
19. ocean just east of North America _____

Word Story One spelling word comes from the Latin word *pacificus*, which meant "peaceful." In 1520 and 1521, Portuguese explorer Ferdinand Magellan sailed a newly discovered ocean. He met mostly calm winds and mild waves, so he gave the ocean this name. Write the name.

20. _____

Family Tree: Asia Compare the spellings, meanings, and pronunciations of the *Asia* words. Then add another *Asia* word to the tree.

Asiatic Sea

21. _____

Eurasia

Asia

Lesson 5: Geography Words
Core Skills Spelling 6, SV 9781419034107

Name: _____   Date: _____

Spelling in Context

The spelling words for this lesson are in the map below. Use the map and the symbols to complete the selection.

Treasures of the World

- On the continent of 🦢 _____, more than $100,000 in stolen cash is buried
  high in the ✖ _____.
                    2

- A Spanish ship carrying $2 million was lost off the coast of Jamaica in the
  ● _____.
      3

- Montezuma may have buried $10 million in gold near Mexico City, as far south as
  ▱ _____.
        4

- A gang threw $180,000 into Mud Lake, Idaho, at the foot of the ❖ _____.
                                                                        5

- The ✠ _____ is the home of $20 million buried by a pirate named
      6
  Jean Lafitte.

- Many tigers live in the countries around the ⬡ _____.
                                                    7

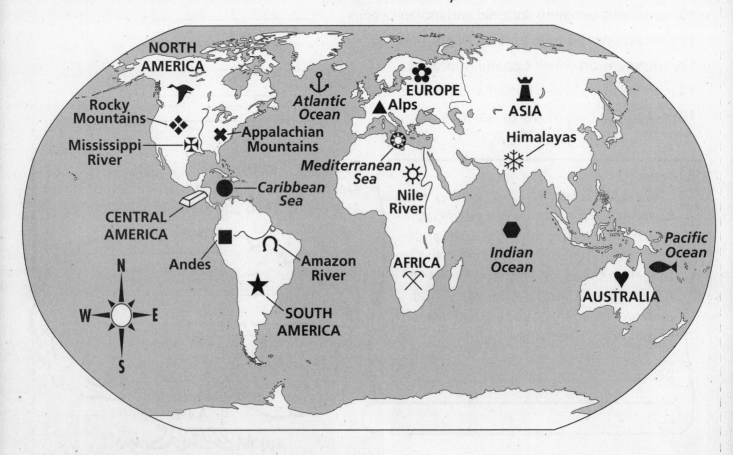

Lesson 5: Geography Words
Core Skills Spelling 6, SV 9781419034107

- Diamonds are found on the continent of ⚒ _____.
  ₈

- The legendary kingdom of El Dorado was supposed to be in Columbia,

  ★ _____, high in the ■ _____ Mountains, which
  ₉   ₁₀

  are west of the ∩ _____.
  ₁₁

- The Suez Canal, one of the seven modern wonders of the world, joins the Red Sea with

  another sea, the ✺ _____.
  ₁₂

- The Loch Ness monster is said to live in Loch Ness, Scotland. The Loch Ness is part of a

  system joining the North Sea and the ⚓ _____ to the south.
  ₁₃

- Try Mt. Everest, high in the ❄ _____ on the continent of
  ₁₄

  ♜ _____, if you want to hunt the Abominable Snowman.
  ₁₅

- The Great Barrier Reef is located off the coast of ♥ _____ in the
  ₁₆

  🐟 _____.
  ₁₇

- Edelweiss, a rare and beautiful flower, grows high in the ▲ _____, which
  ₁₈

  rise from the continent of ❀ _____.
  ₁₉

- Valuable treasures were buried in the pyramids of Egypt near the banks of the

  ☼ _____.
  ₂₀

★ Challenge Yourself ★

Challenge Words

Antarctica
Sahara
Bering Sea
Ganges River

Which Challenge Word fits each clue? Check a dictionary to see if you are right. Then use separate paper to write sentences showing that you understand the meaning of each Challenge Word.

21. This begins in the Himalayas and flows through India.

_____

22. It's sandwiched between the Atlantic Ocean and the Nile River. _____

23. You might go south to this continent to study penguins. _____

24. If you look north from the Aleutian Islands, you might "see" this body of water.

Lesson 6

Words with /ē/

piano

1. e, y, i Words

_____
_____
_____
_____
_____

2. ea, ee, ie, ei Words

_____
_____
_____
_____
_____
_____
_____
_____
_____
_____
_____

3. e-consonant-e Words

_____
_____

4. e-consonant-e and y Word

_____

5. i-consonant-e Word

_____

breeze
complete
brief
degrees
breathing
meter
ceiling
gasoline
piano
memory
scene
succeed
piece
speaker
repeat
receive
liter
library
extremely
increase

Say and Listen

Say each spelling word. Listen for the /ē/ sound you hear in *breeze*.

Think and Sort

Look at the letters in each word. Think about how /ē/ is spelled. Spell each word aloud. How many spelling patterns for /ē/ do you see?

1. Write the five spelling words that have the *e*, *y*, or *i* pattern. Underline the letter that spells /ē/ in each word.

2. Write the eleven spelling words that have the *ea*, *ee*, *ie*, or *ei* pattern. Underline the letters that spell /ē/ in each word.

3. Write the two spelling words that have the *e*-consonant-*e* pattern.

4. Write the one spelling word that has both the *e*-consonant-*e* and the *y* pattern.

5. Write the one spelling word that has the *i*-consonant-*e* pattern.

Use the steps on page 4 to study words that are hard for you.

Spelling Patterns

e	y	i	ea	ee
m**e**ter	memor**y**	p**i**ano	rep**ea**t	br**ee**ze

ie	ei	e-consonant-e	i-consonant-e
br**ie**f	c**ei**ling	compl**ete**	gasol**ine**

Spelling and Meaning

Classifying Write the spelling word that belongs in each group.

1. inches, ounces, _____
2. accomplish, achieve, _____
3. add, expand, _____
4. retell, echo, _____
5. short, condensed, _____
6. thought, remembrance, _____
7. entire, whole, _____
8. accept, acquire, _____
9. very, greatly, _____
10. announcer, presenter, _____
11. eating, sleeping, _____
12. part, segment, _____
13. puff, gust, _____
14. play, act, _____
15. meter, kilogram, _____

Making Connections Complete each sentence by writing the spelling word that goes with the person.

16. A gas station attendant pumps _____.
17. A city employee reads a parking _____.
18. A pianist plays the _____.
19. A librarian helps people find books in the _____.

Word Story One spelling word comes from an old French word, *ciel*, which meant "sky." Today the spelling word names the part of the room that is above everyone's head. Write the word.

20. _____

Family Tree: breathing Breathing is a form of *breathe*. Compare the spellings, meanings, and pronunciations of the *breathe* words. Then add another *breathe* word to the tree.

breathing

21. _____

breath   breathes

breathe

Spelling in Context

Use each spelling word once to complete the selection.

First in Flight

Harriet Quimby was a writer, photographer, and pilot. She became famous for flying an airplane when driving an automobile was still new and exciting. She cut a dashing figure in her purple satin flying costume with a hood rather than a helmet.

Quimby was born in 1875 in Michigan. While still a young girl, she moved with her family to California. She wanted to be an actress. By 1900, however, Quimby was a successful newspaper writer. Although she did not hold any high school or college _____, she had developed an intelligent writing style. She wrote about art and
1
city life. She began to _____ more and more attention for her writing. One
2
_____ of writing that attracted attention was an article about the customs in a
3
section of San Francisco called Chinatown. The article helped _____ readers'
4
interest in and appreciation for the people of Chinatown.

Quimby moved to New York, where she wrote magazine articles. Some of her articles, such as those about household tips and how to find a job, were _____ and to the
5
point. Others were longer features about her travels in foreign countries.

By 1910 Quimby had developed a strong interest in high-speed automobiles. She had bought a car and had written articles on auto repair. Then, after attending an airplane show, she decided to take flying lessons. Learning to fly is like learning to play a flute or a _____, she reasoned; it takes lots and lots of practice. For five weeks, Quimby
6
worked hard. She knew it was important to _____ each step, such as taking off
7
and landing, again and again to make sure she had mastered it.

Quimby learned how to fly in all kinds of weather and could safely land in a light _____ as well as a strong wind. To earn her license, she landed her own plane
8
within an eight-foot, or two-_____, area marked by officials. In 1911 she was
9

the first woman in the United States with a pilot's license.

In the early age of flying, pilots dreamed of crossing the English

Channel. A male pilot had already done so, even though the trip was

considered _____ dangerous. Quimby wanted to be the
                    10

first woman to _____ at this flight.
                      11

The historic flight began at Dover, England. Try to picture the

_____ that day. Everyone was busy. Quimby's assistants
           12

carefully measured the _____ for her fuel tank. Every
                               13

_____ counted. Quimby took off very early in the
         14

morning. Low clouds created a dense cover, or _____,
                                                        15

above the earth. Quimby's heart was pounding. She was

_____ quickly. She knew, though, that she could
         16

_____ the trip. At last the plane touched down in France.
         17

The people cheered. Quimby was the main _____ at her
                                                  18

own celebration rally. She was "a very tired but happy woman," she later

wrote.

Harriet Quimby was a pioneer in the history of flight. Her

_____ will live on. If you'd like to learn more, you can find
         19

books about her at your local _____.
                                      20

| breeze |
| complete |
| brief |
| degrees |
| breathing |
| meter |
| ceiling |
| gasoline |
| piano |
| memory |
| scene |
| succeed |
| piece |
| speaker |
| repeat |
| receive |
| liter |
| library |
| extremely |
| increase |

★ Challenge Yourself ★

Challenge Words

| lethal | careen |
| seacoast | calorie |

What do you think each Challenge Word means? Check a dictionary to see if you are right. Then use separate paper to write sentences showing that you understand the meaning of each Challenge Word.

21. The label warned that the liquid could be **lethal** if swallowed.

22. I saw a sled **careen** from side to side as it raced down the hill.

23. We saw many gulls along the rocky **seacoast** of Maine.

24. To be sure he has energy for sports, Ricardo counts every **calorie** in the foods he eats.

Lesson 7

Words with /ŭ/

flood

1. *u* Words

_____
_____
_____
_____
_____
_____
_____
_____
_____

2. *o* Words

_____
_____
_____
_____

3. *ou* Words

_____
_____
_____
_____
_____
_____

4. *oo* Word

_____

thumb
struggle
umbrella
flood
touch
government
tongue
trouble
double
justice
difficult
compass
enough
crumb
among
cousin
tough
discuss
plumber
result

Say and Listen

Say each spelling word. Listen for the /ŭ/ sound you hear in *thumb*.

Think and Sort

Look at the letters in each word. Think about how /ŭ/ is spelled. Spell each word aloud.

How many spelling patterns for /ŭ/ do you see?

1. Write the nine spelling words that have the *u* pattern.

2. Write the four spelling words that have the *o* pattern.

3. Write the six spelling words that have the *ou* pattern.

4. Write the one spelling word that has the *oo* pattern.

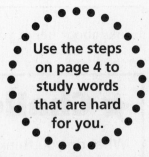

Use the steps on page 4 to study words that are hard for you.

Spelling Patterns

u	**o**	**ou**	**oo**
th**u**mb	am**o**ng	t**ou**ch	fl**oo**d

Spelling and Meaning

Clues Write the spelling word for each clue.

1. This helps people to find their way. _____
2. This is very useful in rainy weather. _____
3. Congress is part of this. _____
4. This word means *sufficient*. _____
5. This word names a relative. _____
6. This word means the opposite of *easy*. _____
7. People do this when they share ideas. _____
8. This word means the same as *outcome*. _____
9. This can be the remains of a piece of toast. _____
10. People want this in a court of law. _____
11. A frog catches flies with this. _____

Rhymes Write the spelling word that completes each sentence and rhymes with the underlined word.

12. The lights were <u>strung</u> _____ the trees in the back yard.
13. The _____ left a lot of <u>mud</u> in the cellar.
14. I'll blow a <u>bubble</u> that is _____ the size of yours!
15. It's a _____ to <u>juggle</u> four balls at once.
16. My _____ was <u>numb</u> from the cold.
17. The man's <u>gruff</u> voice makes him seem _____.
18. <u>Double</u> vision is _____ for a driver.
19. Do not _____ my <u>crutch</u> when I am walking.

Word Story One of the spelling words used to be *plumbum*, which meant "lead." The ancient Romans used lead pipes to carry water. The spelling word refers to a person who puts in new water pipes and repairs old ones. Write the word.

20. _____

Family Tree: *crumb* Compare the spellings, meanings, and pronunciations of the *crumb* words. Then add another *crumb* word to the tree.

crumble

21. _____

crumbly   crumbs

crumb

Spelling in Context

Use each spelling word once to complete the story.

The Case of the Hungry Gopher

"That muffin was delicious!" exclaimed seven-year-old Alex as he wiped a

_____ off his chin. "Aunt Delia is a great cook!" He glanced at his

1

_____, Julia.

2

"You've got a piece of blueberry on your lip," said thirteen-year-old Julia. Alex licked it with

his _____. "I've had _____ to eat," he said. "Let's do

3   4

something exciting."

"What do you have in mind?" asked Julia.

"Why don't we play like we're detectives?" he asked excitedly. "Or maybe we can pretend

we're spies and make up secret messages."

"I have an idea," said Julia. "Let's suppose that we are special agents for the federal

_____ and are tracking a spy. We'll catch the spy and bring the person to

5

_____."

6

Aunt Delia interrupted the two as she came up the basement stairs. "Where's Uncle Tomas?"

she asked. "Tomas! Tomas!" she shouted. "Come here on the _____! We've got

7

water _____. If we don't call a _____ right away, we'll have a

8   9

_____ in the basement!" Uncle Tomas was nowhere to be found.

10

Alex and Julia looked at each other. "Here's our chance to be detectives," Alex whispered.

The two didn't have to _____ what to do. They sprang into action. First Julia

11

got a couple of raincoats and a large old _____ from the closet. The rain gear

12

would help in case water was pouring from the basement ceiling.

Alex grabbed his special _____ from a cabinet drawer. "This compass

13

glows in the dark," he said. "It will help us find our way in case we get lost. Can you find a

flashlight, Julia? It's _____ to see down there."

14

Julia opened a drawer and found an old flashlight. She clicked it on with her

www.harcourtschoolsupply.com
32
Lesson 7: Words with /ŭ/
Core Skills Spelling 6, SV 9781419034107

_____. The flashlight immediately responded to her
15

_____ and shone brightly. The private investigators were
16

ready to go to work.

Water pooled on the basement floor, but the ceiling was dry. Julia had to

_____ to fold up the old umbrella. She and Alex finally
17

spotted a trickle of water coming from a window. Julia shone the flashlight

toward the window. The light revealed a pair of greenish eyes and a set of

whiskers _____ some flowers outside. Then the eyes
18

disappeared.

Alex and Julia raced upstairs and around to the side of the house. Alex

spotted a garden hose. By that time, both Uncle Tomas and a plumber had

arrived. Alex showed them the garden hose. "Look," he said. "Something has

gnawed a hole in the hose. The _____ was water in the
19

basement."

"Yes," said Aunt Delia, "and I bet that 'something' is the same gopher

that's eaten half the vegetables in our garden, too."

"Good job on a _____ case," Julia said to Alex.
20

"You're a great detective."

thumb
struggle
umbrella
flood
touch
government
tongue
trouble
double
justice
difficult
compass
enough
crumb
among
cousin
tough
discuss
plumber
result

★ Challenge Yourself ★

Challenge Words

wonderment
roughness
impulsive
junction

Use a dictionary to answer these questions. Then use separate paper to write sentences showing that you understand the meaning of each Challenge Word.

21. Would a young child watch a breathtaking fireworks display in **wonderment**? _____

22. Can you smooth a board's **roughness** by sanding it? _____

23. Would an **impulsive** person think long and hard before making a major purchase, such as buying a car? _____

24. Could a train cross over to another track at a railway **junction**? _____

Lesson 8

Words with /yo͞o/ or /o͞o/

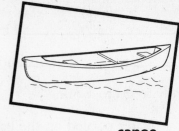

canoe

Spelling Word List

refuse
glue
student
nuisance
coupon
renew
human
canoe
improvement
smooth
beautiful
rude
juice
through
threw
clue
humor
ruin
pollute
cruel

1. *oo, u* Words

_____
_____
_____
_____
_____
_____

2. *ew, ue, u*-consonant-*e* Words

_____
_____
_____
_____
_____
_____
_____

3. *ou, oe, o*-consonant-*e* Words

_____
_____
_____
_____

4. *ui, eau* Words

_____
_____
_____

Say and Listen

Say each spelling word. Listen for the /o͞o/ sound you hear in *refuse* and *glue*.

Think and Sort

All of the spelling words have the /o͞o/ sound. In *refuse* and some other /o͞o/ words, /y/ is pronounced before the /o͞o/.

Look at the letters in each spelling word. Think about how /o͞o/ or /yo͞o/ is spelled. Spell each word aloud.

1. Write the six words that have the *oo* or *u* pattern.

2. Write the seven words that have the *ew, ue,* or *u*-consonant-*e* pattern.

3. Write the four words that have the *ou, oe,* or *o*-consonant-*e* pattern.

4. Write the three words that have the *ui* or *eau* pattern.

Use the steps on page 4 to study words that are hard for you.

Spelling Patterns

oo sm**oo**th	**u** h**u**mor	**ew** thr**ew**	**ue** gl**ue**
u-consonant-**e** ref**use**		**ou** thr**ou**gh	**oe** can**oe**
o-consonant-**e** impr**ove**ment		**ui** j**ui**ce	**eau** b**eau**tiful

Spelling and Meaning

Analogies Write the spelling word that completes each analogy.

1. *Bicycle* is to *motorcycle* as _____ is to *motorboat*.

2. *Potato* is to *chip* as *apple* is to _____.

3. *Tremble* is to *anger* as *laugh* is to _____.

4. *Automobile* is to *car* as _____ is to *person*.

5. *Melt* is to *freeze* as *clean* is to _____.

6. *Destruction* is to *crush* as _____ is to *bother*.

7. *Unsightly* is to *ugly* as *gorgeous* is to _____.

8. *Bridge* is to *over* as *tunnel* is to _____.

9. *Improve* is to _____ as *manage* is to *management*.

10. *Discount* is to _____ as *admittance* is to *ticket*.

Synonyms Complete each sentence with the spelling word that is a synonym of the underlined word.

11. Cold lemonade will <u>refresh</u> you and _____ your energy.

12. Marissa's skin is as _____ and <u>silky</u> as a baby's.

13. That _____ is a very strong <u>adhesive</u>.

14. Sara <u>tossed</u> the ball to Ling, who _____ it to Miguel.

15. Although he was _____ to us, we were not <u>impolite</u> to him.

16. We <u>decline</u> your offer and _____ to play.

17. His _____ actions were met with a <u>vicious</u> growl.

18. Ann's <u>hint</u> was the _____ that solved the mystery.

19. A bad fire can <u>destroy</u> property and _____ lives.

Word Story One spelling word comes from the Latin word *studere*, which meant "to study." Today we use the spelling word to refer to someone who goes to school. It can also refer to someone who is eager to know and learn. Write the word.

20. _____

Family Tree: *human* Compare the spellings, meanings, and pronunciations of the *human* words Then add another *human* word to the tree.

humanitarian

21. _____

humanity   humans

human

Lesson 8: Words with /yŏŏ/ or /ŏŏ/
Core Skills Spelling 6, SV 9781419034107

Spelling in Context

Use each spelling word once to complete the story.

To the Rescue

This year our science class took a different kind of field trip. We helped clean up trash along the banks of Silver River. Mr. Karas, our science teacher, had a _____ 1 for free pizza at a local restaurant. He said that our class could have a pizza party if we helped to clean up the river. We decided that it was an offer too good to _____ 2. Not one _____ 3 in the class wanted to miss the fun.

It was a _____ 4 spring morning. The sun shone brightly _____ 5 the trees and reflected off the water. As we worked, Mr. Karas talked. "This river has undergone a vast _____ 6 during the past ten years," he said. "The river and all the land along it were once near _____ 7 because a factory began to _____ 8 the water. The factory made a quick-drying, very strong _____ 9. It was a good product, but it was made with many chemicals that killed both plants and animals."

"Polluting the water is a _____ 10 thing to do to the fish and birds that live here," Angela said.

"Things are much better, though," Mr. Karas continued. "The fish population has begun to _____ 11 itself."

"Excuse me, Mr. Karas," Josh said excitedly. "I don't mean to be _____ 12, but look over there!" Josh pointed to a yellow _____ 13 in the middle of the river. A young man and woman were paddling frantically, trying hard to stay afloat.

Mr. Karas turned to look where Josh was pointing. "Their boat must be leaking!" he cried. He sent Andy to the bus to find a piece of rope. Andy returned in an instant.

In the meantime I waved my arms to get the boaters' attention. I wanted to give them some _____ 14 that help was on the way.

"No time to lose!" cried Mr. Karas as he waded into the water. The water near the bank was calm and _____15_____. Out in the middle, though, the currents ran swiftly. Mr. Karas _____16_____ the rope to the canoers, but it fell short.

We needed something heavy. I reached in my lunch box and pulled out a large bottle of fruit _____17_____. Mr. Karas tied the rope to the bottle and tossed it toward the canoe. This time the rope reached the canoe, and the young woman grabbed it. In no time she and the man stood safely on land.

The young couple could not thank us enough. "We're really glad that you were here to rescue us," they said. "Please forgive us for being such a _____18_____."

"We're glad we could help," we all replied. Then the couple joined us at the restaurant for our pizza party. All of us were in good _____19_____, and we had a great time celebrating the rescue. After all, it's _____20_____ nature to want to help and to feel good about it when you do.

refuse
glue
student
nuisance
coupon
renew
human
canoe
improvement
smooth
beautiful
rude
juice
through
threw
clue
humor
ruin
pollute
cruel

★ Challenge Yourself ★

Challenge Words

neutral	boutique
intrude	tuition

Write the Challenge Word for each clue. Check a dictionary to see if you are right. Then use separate paper to write sentences showing that you understand the meaning of each Challenge Word.

21. You could buy fancy, expensive clothes at this place. _____

22. This is what college students pay to attend school. _____

23. If you don't favor either side in an argument, you are this. _____

24. If you interrupt a private conversation, you are said to do this. _____

Lesson 8: Words with /yoo/ or /oo/
Core Skills Spelling 6, SV 9781419034107

Name: _____   Date: _____

Lesson 9 Plural Words

wolves

Spelling word list

1. -s Plurals
_____
_____
_____
_____

2. -es Plurals with No Base Word Changes
_____
_____
_____
_____
_____

3. -es Plurals with Base Word Changes
_____
_____
_____
_____
_____
_____
_____
_____
_____
_____
_____

knives
loaves
tomatoes
mysteries
canoes
memories
halves
mosquitoes
holidays
industries
wolves
heroes
voyages
countries
bakeries
potatoes
pianos
factories
echoes
libraries

Say and Listen

Say the spelling words. Listen to the ending sounds.

Think and Sort

All of the spelling words are plurals. A **base word** is a word to which prefixes, suffixes, and word endings can be added to form new words. Most plurals are formed by adding -s to the base word. Other plurals are formed by adding -es. The spelling of some base words changes when -es is added.

bakery + es = baker**ies**   wolf + es = wol**ves**

Look at the letters in each word. Think about how each plural is formed. Spell each word aloud.

1. Write the four spelling words formed by adding -s to the base word.

2. Write the five -es spelling words with no changes in the base word.

3. Write the eleven -es spelling words with changes in the base word.

Use the steps on page 4 to study words that are hard for you.

Spelling Patterns

-s	-es		
canoe**s**	echo**es**	baker**ies**	wol**ves**

Spelling and Meaning

Definitions   Write the spelling word for each definition.

1. repeated sounds bouncing off something   _____
2. things that cannot be explained   _____
3. people known for courage   _____
4. nations or states   _____
5. things that are remembered   _____
6. bread baked in large pieces   _____
7. groups of businesses   _____
8. underground stems eaten as vegetables   _____
9. two equal parts of a whole   _____

Clues   Write the spelling word for each clue.

10. These are often eaten in salads.   _____
11. Another word for this is *journeys*.   _____
12. These are places where cars are manufactured.   _____
13. Pianists play these.   _____
14. These flying insects can be annoying.   _____
15. People use paddles to move these.   _____
16. These places sell pastries.   _____
17. People borrow books at these places.   _____
18. People use these to cut bread.   _____
19. These animals are related to dogs.   _____

Word Story   One spelling word comes from *holigdaeg*, which meant "holy day." Now the spelling word names any day of celebration and freedom from work. Write the plural form of this word.

20. _____

Family Tree: memories   *Memories* is a form of *memory*. Compare the spellings, meanings, and pronunciations of the *memory* words. Then add another *memory* word to the tree.

memories

21. _____

memorable   memorial

memory

Spelling in Context

Use each spelling word once to complete the selection.

Paul Bunyan:
An American Folk Hero

Most _____ have their own popular folk _____. A

1
                                                                2

whole series of tall tales has been written about Paul Bunyan, one of the most famous folk

heroes in the United States. Paul was an enormous fellow who grew up to be a number-one

lumberjack. Paul's constant companion was Babe, a blue ox. Babe was so big that seven ax

handles could fit between his eyes. Paul split whole trees into two pieces with one stroke and

carried the _____ of the trees to lumber _____. Paul and

       3   4

Babe kept all of these factories in the country supplied with wood. In fact, because of Paul,

logging became one of the most important _____ in our country at that

                                              5

time. Despite some _____ surrounding Paul Bunyan's life, books in

                       6

_____ tell a great deal

       7

about Paul and Babe. Here's a tale you may

not have heard.

   One morning Paul and Babe left

a logging camp in Maine for a short

stroll. As they headed west, all the

_____ and deer ran to

       8

escape the thundering sound of Paul and

Babe's footsteps. Paul laughed and laughed as

they walked. The _____ of

                   9

his laughter rolled through the valleys like

thunder. By midmorning they'd walked 1,200

miles and had reached the Mississippi River.

40

Lesson 9: Plural Words
Core Skills Spelling 6, SV 9781419034107

Paul and Babe were quite hungry, so they stopped at a logging camp to eat. Everyone was proud to have Paul Bunyan as a guest. Bakers in all the nearby _____ started to make extra bread. Paul could fit 17
10
_____ on the tip of his tongue. The cook's helpers peeled
11
200 pounds of _____ to bake and mash. They used so many
12
_____ to make a ton of ketchup that they had to plant a
13
whole new crop. Everyone helped carve forks and _____
14
big enough to hold a mouthful for Paul. Paul and Babe used
_____ from the river as teacups. Some insects were
15
attracted by all the food. Paul's skin was so thick, however, that the
_____ got concussions trying to bite him.
16
The logging folks began to sing to Babe. They pounded on the keys of
23 _____ to make the music loud enough for him to hear.
17
They sang love songs, songs about sailors and sea _____,
18
and the lumberjack songs "Moosehead Lake" and "The Frozen Logger."
Soon it was time to leave, and Paul and Babe headed back to Maine. The
Mississippi loggers decided to keep their fond _____ of
19
Paul and Babe's visit alive by making that day into one of the most popular
_____ in the camp.
20

knives
loaves
tomatoes
mysteries
canoes
memories
halves
mosquitoes
holidays
industries
wolves
heroes
voyages
countries
bakeries
potatoes
pianos
factories
echoes
libraries

★ Challenge Yourself ★

Challenge Words

rosebushes
nationalities
wharves
fisheries

Use a dictionary to answer these questions. Then use separate paper to write sentences showing that you understand the meaning of each Challenge Word.

21. Could bees be found in a garden of **rosebushes**?

_____

22. Does the world contain people of all **nationalities**? _____

23. Could you see boats and ships in a city with **wharves**? _____

24. Would it make sense to have **fisheries** in places that have no water?

_____

Lesson 10

Words with /əl/

castle

1. *al* Words

_____
_____
_____
_____
_____
_____

2. *el* Words

_____
_____
_____
_____

3. *le* Words

_____
_____
_____
_____
_____
_____
_____
_____
_____

nickel
several
wrestle
natural
muscle
vegetable
hospital
grumble
castle
carnival
bicycle
general
example
whistle
principal
principle
novel
label
tunnel
usually

Say and Listen

Say each spelling word. Listen for the /əl/ sounds you hear at the end of *nickel*.

Think and Sort

Look at the letters in each word. Think about how /əl/ is spelled. Spell each word aloud.

How many spelling patterns for /əl/ do you see?

1. Write the seven spelling words that have the *al* pattern.

2. Write the four spelling words that have the *el* pattern.

3. Write the nine spelling words that have the *le* pattern.

Use the steps on page 4 to study words that are hard for you.

Spelling Patterns

al gener**al**	**el** nick**el**	**le** mus**cle**

Spelling and Meaning

Classifying Write the spelling word that belongs in each group.

1. circus, fair, _____
2. sample, model, _____
3. tag, sticker, _____
4. penny, _____, dime
5. complain, mutter, _____
6. lieutenant, captain, _____
7. few, some, _____
8. seldom, sometimes, _____
9. mansion, palace, _____
10. meat, grain, _____
11. student, teacher, _____
12. real, pure, _____

Making Connections Complete each sentence by writing the spelling word that goes with the person or persons.

13. The coach showed his team the correct way to _____.
14. The famous author wrote a new _____.
15. The body builder developed his _____ tone.
16. Doctors and nurses often work in a _____.
17. The miners worked all day in the dark _____.
18. A cyclist rides a _____.
19. The referee blew her _____ at the end of the game.

Word Story   One spelling word comes from the Latin word *princeps*, which meant "something of great importance." Today the spelling word means "basic or fundamental law." Write the word.

20. _____

Family Tree: *hospital* Compare the spellings, meanings, and pronunciations of the *hospital* words. Then add another *hospital* word to the tree.

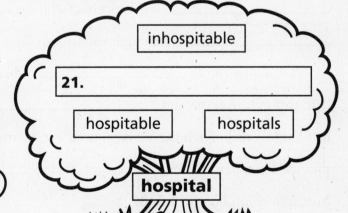

inhospitable

21.

hospitable   hospitals

hospital

Spelling in Context

Use each spelling word once to complete the selection.

The Iron Road

In 1862 the U. S. Congress decided to build a railroad that would run _____ 1 thousand miles across the whole United States. It was called the Transcontinental Railroad. The _____ 2 population supported the plan, but everyone knew the actual building of the railroad would be difficult. Two companies took responsibility for the construction. The Central Pacific built from the West. The Union Pacific built from the East.

One of the biggest problems was the steep Sierra Nevada mountain range in California. There weren't enough _____ 3 passages through the mountains, so somehow a path had to be built. While some engineers would _____ 4 and complain that the task was impossible, a bright young man came up with the _____ 5 idea of digging and blasting out a path. His name was Theodore Judah, and he was the founder of the Central Pacific.

Now that the how was answered, the question was who was going to do it. The answer came in the form of more than 10,000 workers from China. They provided the _____ 6, or most important, labor force for the Central Pacific.

The Chinese workers used _____ 7 power to get the job done. For _____ 8, workers chiseled ledges in cliffs. Some used hand drills to _____ 9 through mountains. The work was difficult and slow.

Living by the _____ 10 of hard work, the Chinese worked day and night to drill through iron ore and _____ 11 deposits. Granite was _____ 12 too hard to drill. Then the workers used explosives to blast through the rock. The explosives were provided by chemists. Part of their job was to _____ 13 the explosives with good instructions on how to handle them.

The winters were hard. The workers had to _____

14

with high winds and snow. They built huts to keep warm. Even a king's

_____ with thick stone walls wouldn't have kept out the

15

chilling winds. There was no _____ nearby to treat injuries.

16

Food was hauled in by sled. A typical worker's meal included fish, rice, and a

_____ such as pea pods. The food helped the workers stay

17

healthy.

In 1869 the great iron railroad was finally completed. A train from the

Central Pacific and another from the Union Pacific, each blowing its

_____, met in Promontory, Utah. There the last spike in the

18

track was hammered into place. At the same time, Californians had a two-day-

long _____ with fireworks. After many years, thousands of

19

miles, and lots of hard work, they celebrated the completion of the railroad.

With the completion of the mighty Transcontinental Railroad, the

westward expansion began. Today the West is the home of major cities and

industries. It is also the home of ski lodges, campgrounds, and hiking and

_____ trails for all people to enjoy. What seemed like an

20

impossible task turned out to be a great success.

nickel
several
wrestle
natural
muscle
vegetable
hospital
grumble
castle
carnival
bicycle
general
example
whistle
principal
principle
novel
label
tunnel
usually

★ Challenge Yourself ★

Challenge Words

| mythical | novelty |
| enamel | residential |

What do you think each Challenge Word means? Check a dictionary to see if you are right. Then use separate paper to write sentences showing that you understand the meaning of each Challenge Word.

21. The **mythical** beast had the head of a lion, the body of a horse, and the tail of a pig.

22. When the **novelty** of a May snowstorm wore off, we went inside to warm up.

23. The **enamel** on the surface of the old stove was chipped and peeling.

24. Their new home is in a quiet **residential** part of the city.

Lesson 11

Words with /ĭ/

experiment

1. *i* Words
_____
_____
_____
_____
_____
_____

2. *y* Words
_____
_____
_____

3. *e* Words
_____
_____

4. Words with More Than One Pattern
_____
_____
_____
_____
_____
_____

million
business
electric
rhythm
margarine
opinion
myth
brilliant
spinach
equipment
gymnastic
definite
select
system
relative
witness
detective
experiment
scissors
liquid

Say and Listen

Say each spelling word. Listen for the /ĭ/ sound you hear in *million*.

Think and Sort

Look at the letters in each word. Think about how /ĭ/ is spelled. Spell each word aloud.

How many spelling patterns for /ĭ/ do you see? Which words contain more than one spelling pattern for /ĭ/?

1. Write the eight spelling words with only the *i* pattern.

2. Write the three spelling words with only the *y* pattern.

3. Write the two spelling words with only the *e* pattern.

4. Write the seven spelling words with more than one spelling pattern for /ĭ/. Underline the letters that spell /ĭ/ in each word.

Use the steps on page 4 to study words that are hard for you.

Spelling Patterns

i	**y**	**e**	**i a**	**u e**
m**i**llion	m**y**th	s**e**lect	sp**i**n**a**ch	b**u**sin**e**ss

Spelling and Meaning

Analogies   Write the spelling word that completes each analogy.

1. *Cut* is to _____ as *write* is to *pencil*.

2. *Magenta* is to *color* as _____ is to *number*.

3. *Rock* is to a *solid* as *water* is to _____.

4. *Vegetable* is to _____ as *fruit* is to *apple*.

5. *Jam* is to *jelly* as *butter* is to _____.

6. *Choose* is to _____ as *purchase* is to *buy*.

7. *Parent* is to *mother* as _____ is to *cousin*.

8. *Mend* is to *repair* as *smart* is to _____.

9. *Beat* is to _____ as *tune* is to *melody*.

Clues   Write the spelling word for each clue.

10. This is a method of doing something. _____

11. This person sees a crime take place. _____

12. This story tries to explain something in nature. _____

13. This word describes exercises involving stunts on mats and bars. _____

14. This person investigates crimes. _____

15. This is the making, buying, and selling of goods. _____

16. You might perform this in science class. _____

17. This is the opposite of *fact*. _____

18. *Specific* and *sure* are synonyms for this word. _____

19. These are all the things that help you do a specific job. _____

Word Story   One spelling word comes from the ancient Greek word *elektor*, which meant "the beaming sun." Write the word.

20. _____

Family Tree: *select*   Compare the spellings, meanings, and pronunciations of the *select* words. Then add another *select* word to the tree.

selective

21. _____

selectively   selected

select

Spelling in Context

Use each spelling word once to complete the story.

A Matter of Myth

"One thing is absolutely _____1_____," said Meg with a groan as she pushed

down the lever on the _____2_____ toaster. "Boys just can't take care of kids as well as

girls can!"

"That's not true," said Jeff. "Aren't you the one who's always saying it's a

_____3_____ that a girl can't be a mechanic or a ballplayer or a private

_____4_____? Now that a few guys have gotten together to form the Boys' Baby-

Sitting Business, you girls forget about equal rights! If girls can do anything boys can do, how

come it doesn't work the other way around? What kind of _____5_____ is that?"

"I for one don't think the BBB is such a _____6_____ idea," said his sister with a

smug smile as she spread _____7_____ on her toast. Meg flicked on the radio and

began dancing to the _____8_____ of the music. She wasn't going to discuss it any

longer.

Later, on the way to school, both Jeff and Meg were silent. Jeff had been expecting Meg to

help the BBB by passing out _____9_____ cards to her classmates who had little

brothers and sisters. After all, when Meg's _____10_____ team needed new

_____11_____, didn't he help them raise money? By the time they arrived at school,

Jeff wished Meg weren't his sister or even a distant _____12_____.

In science class Meg began working on an _____13_____. The object was to see

how much _____14_____ could be made by turning steam back into water. Meg's best

friend, Madeline, sent her a note. She asked her for a pair of _____15_____ to cut out a

label. At the bottom of the note, Madeline added a P.S. It read, "Isn't it great that the boys have a

baby-sitting business?"

"No, in my _____16_____ it's a dumb idea!" Meg hastily wrote back.

Madeline was puzzled. At lunch the two girls went through the cafeteria line to _____ some sandwiches and two _____ salads. As soon as they found a table, Madeline asked what the note meant.

"Boys can't be good sitters," Meg explained. "Taking care of kids comes naturally to girls. It would take a _____ boys to look after one kid. Boys just don't know what to do."

"Oh, yes they do!" said Madeline. "Yesterday Aunt Clara needed someone to take care of Roberto. I told her to ask Jim Grant. Jim did a great job as a baby sitter. I was a _____ to it. Roberto really liked him, too."

Thoughtfully Meg propped her chin in her hands. Maybe Jeff was right. Maybe the BBB wasn't such a dumb idea. Maybe if girls could do things boys do, boys could do things girls do. Maybe some of her ideas *were* myths!

Word list (spiral notepad):

- million
- business
- electric
- rhythm
- margarine
- opinion
- myth
- brilliant
- spinach
- equipment
- gymnastic
- definite
- select
- system
- relative
- witness
- detective
- experiment
- scissors
- liquid

★ Challenge Yourself ★

Challenge Words

forfeit
integrate
immortality
crystallized

What do you think each Challenge Word means? Check a dictionary to see if you are right. Then use separate paper to write sentences showing that you understand the meaning of each Challenge Word.

21. If you are gone when we call your name, you will **forfeit** your turn.

22. Ping tried to **integrate** his teacher's ideas into his story.

23. The writer achieved **immortality** through her popular books.

24. On the cold winter morning, drops of water **crystallized** into ice on the windowpane.

Lesson 12
More Words with /ĭ/

chocolate

1. a-consonant-e Words

_____
_____
_____
_____
_____
_____
_____
_____
_____
_____
_____
_____
_____
_____
_____
_____
_____
_____

2. i and a-consonant-e Words

_____
_____

luggage
cabbage
private
percentage
sausage
advantage
beverage
passage
message
immediate
storage
image
desperate
courage
average
chocolate
pirate
accurate
language
fortunate

Say and Listen
Say each spelling word. Listen for the /ĭ/ sound you hear in *luggage*.

Think and Sort
Look at the letters in each word. Think about how /ĭ/ is spelled. Spell each word aloud.

How many spelling patterns for /ĭ/ do you see? Which words contain more than one spelling pattern for /ĭ/?

1. Write the eighteen spelling words that have only the *a-consonant-e* pattern.

2. Write the two spelling words that have the *i* and *a-consonant-e* patterns. Underline the letters that spell /ĭ/ in each word.

Use the steps on page 4 to study words that are hard for you.

Spelling Patterns

a-consonant-e	i and a-consonant-e
lugg**age**	**i**m**age**

Spelling and Meaning

Synonyms Write the spelling word that is a synonym for each word below.

1. suitcases   _____
2. drink   _____
3. lucky   _____
4. correct   _____
5. personal   _____
6. typical   _____
7. statement   _____

Definitions Write the spelling word for each definition.

8. words spoken and understood by a group   _____
9. a narrow path   _____
10. a place for keeping things   _____
11. a leafy light-green vegetable   _____
12. a mental picture   _____
13. taking place at once   _____
14. someone who lives by robbing ships   _____
15. a better position   _____
16. a food made from cacao seeds   _____
17. a spicy meat mixture shaped like a frankfurter   _____
18. in an almost hopeless situation   _____
19. portion of a whole   _____

Word Story One spelling word originally comes from *cor*, a Latin word that meant "heart." People believed the heart was responsible for love and bravery. The word came into modern English through the Middle English word *corage*. Write the word used today.

20. _____

Family Tree: *image* Compare the spellings, meanings, and pronunciations of the *image* words. Then add another *image* word to the tree.

imaginative

21.

imagine   imaginary

image

Name: _____   Date: _____

The Case of the Pirate's Coin

1311 Meadows Lane

Three Falls, ME 10312

November 16

Dear Will,

    I thought I would take _____ of this free moment and write you a

1

letter. Did you get my _____ saying that I was going to spend a few days

2

at my Aunt Hattie's in Maine? It took a little _____, but I handled the

3

plane ride like a pro!

    My Aunt Hattie met me at the airport and put my _____ into her

4

truck. Boy, was I surprised to see what Maine is like. It's nothing like the

_____ I had of it. We drove through some big forests on the way to Aunt

5

Hattie's cottage. It sits by a secluded _____ lake that's miles from the main

6

highway.

    At first I thought this was going to be an _____ visit. But listen to

7

what happened this morning! Aunt Hattie discovered she'd lost a valuable coin from her

collection. She said she'd bought it from another collector. He said that the coin came from

a treasure chest hidden by a _____ hundreds of years ago.

8

    Aunt Hattie was frantically looking for the missing coin. She was becoming

_____. It was quite _____ that I was there to help out.

9   **10**

I told her about our detective work back home. That gave her hope. She wanted an

_____ investigation. We began to search the house. We even looked along

11

the narrow _____ from the house to the barn. Guess
₁₂

what I saw in the _____ room. There were piles and
₁₃

piles of detective magazines stacked up to the ceiling. A large

_____ of them were written in English, but there
₁₄

were several in French, Italian, and even the Greek

_____. I know what I can do if I get bored!
₁₅

    I asked my aunt to give an _____ account of
₁₆

how she'd spent her morning. Her answer led us to the tool shed. Sure

enough, we found the coin near some clay pots. It had fallen out of

her pocket. (Why did she put a coin that was supposed to be 200 years

old in her pocket in the first place?)

    Well, I have to go to the store now. Aunt Hattie wants to get

_____ and pork _____ for dinner.
₁₇   ₁₈

I get to decide on the _____.
₁₉

    I think I'll get _____ milk.
₂₀

                        Write back,

                        Claudia

Word list (spiral notepad):

- luggage
- cabbage
- private
- percentage
- sausage
- advantage
- beverage
- passage
- message
- immediate
- storage
- image
- desperate
- courage
- average
- chocolate
- pirate
- accurate
- language
- fortunate

★ Challenge Yourself ★

Challenge Words

inadequate
pomegranate
appendage
cartilage

Use a dictionary to answer these questions. Then use separate paper to write sentences showing that you understand the meaning of each Challenge Word.

21. Is twenty dollars an **inadequate** amount of money for
lunch at your school? _____

22. Is **pomegranate** a rock used to make statues like those found in ancient
Greece and Rome? _____

23. Is the arm an example of an **appendage** of the body? _____

24. Is **cartilage** found inside the human ear and nose? _____

Lesson 13
Words with /ī/

violin

1. *i*-consonant-*e* Words
_____
_____
_____
_____
_____
_____
_____
_____

2. *y* Words
_____
_____
_____

3. *i* Words
_____
_____
_____
_____
_____
_____
_____

4. *igh* Word
_____

5. *y*-consonant-*e* Word
_____

strike
surprise
style
science
violin
survive
realize
violet
notify
appetite
sigh
describe
deny
advertise
recognize
choir
silence
design
apply
assign

Say and Listen
Say each spelling word. Listen for the /ī/ sound you hear in *strike*.

Think and Sort
Look at the letters in each word. Think about how /ī/ is spelled. Spell each word aloud.

How many spelling patterns for /ī/ do you see?

1. Write the eight spelling words with the *i*-consonant-*e* pattern.

2. Write the three spelling words with the *y* pattern.

3. Write the seven spelling words with the *i* pattern.

4. Write the one spelling word with the *igh* pattern.

5. Write the one spelling word with the *y*-consonant-*e* pattern.

Use the steps on page 4 to study words that are hard for you.

Spelling Patterns

i-consonant-*e*	*y*	*i*
stri**ke**	den**y**	**sci**ence

igh	**y**-consonant-*e*	
s**igh**	st**yle**	

www.harcourtschoolsupply.com
54
Lesson 13: Words with /ī/
Core Skills Spelling 6, SV 9781419034107

Spelling and Meaning

Classifying   Write the spelling word that belongs in each group.

1. guitar, cello, _____

2. hunger, craving, _____

3. history, math, _____

4. tell, inform, _____

5. purple, blue, _____

6. understand, discover, _____

7. quiet, hush, _____

8. plan, create, _____

9. appoint, designate, _____

10. shock, astonish, _____

11. remain, outlast, _____

12. identify, recall, _____

Rhymes   Write the spelling word that completes each sentence and rhymes with the underlined word.

13. Pilots must _____ for a license to <u>fly</u>.

14. The miners would <u>like</u> to _____ gold.

15. Can you _____ how that ancient <u>tribe</u> lived?

16. Can we <u>hire</u> a _____ to sing at the assembly?

17. I like that _____ of floor <u>tile</u>.

18. Julia looked up at the <u>sky</u> with a wishful _____.

19. Don't <u>try</u> to _____ that it was your idea.

Word Story   One spelling word describes what billboards and commercials do. The word comes from the Latin word *advertere*, which meant "turn toward." Advertisers try to persuade you to "turn toward" their product. Write the word.

20. _____

Family Tree: *survive*   Compare the spellings, meanings, and pronunciations of the *survive* words. Then add another *survive* word to the tree.

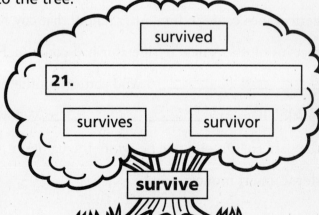

survived

21.

survives   survivor

survive

Spelling in Context

Use each spelling word once to complete the story.

Sydney Has the Last Laugh

The clock outside school began to _____ 1 _____ 10 o'clock. Abe heaved a big

_____ 2 _____ and looked down at his old tennis shoes. At 7 o'clock that night he

would have to be back for the school dance. Abe hated dancing. It just wasn't his

_____ 3 _____. "I'll never _____ 4 _____ the evening," he thought while

working on his experiment in _____ 5 _____ class. "But if I don't go, Mike and Sydney

and all my other friends will never let me forget it."

Just then, Sydney poked him. "You just spilled something," she said. "Are you thinking about

the dance tonight?"

"What should I say to her?" he thought. "Should I _____ 6 _____ that I was

thinking about the dance?" Abe didn't listen as Sydney began to _____ 7 _____ the

events that were planned for the evening. There was an awkward _____ 8 _____. When

the bell rang, he was saved for the moment.

The rest of the day went much too quickly for him. Abe saw Sydney once again during

_____ 9 _____ rehearsal. He made sure their eyes didn't meet when the music teacher

decided to _____ 10 _____ her a seat next to him. More than once he thought about

going to _____ 11 _____ the principal that he would be transferring to another school.

It was while Abe was tuning his _____ 12 _____ during orchestra practice that the

perfect idea came to him. After school that day, he ran straight home and found the giant carton

that his mother's new refrigerator had come in. He used some marking pens to

_____ 13 _____ a wild pattern on the box. Then he found a brush and some paints and

quickly began to _____ 14 _____ yellow, red, and _____ 15 _____ paint to fill in

the pattern. On one side he wrote the names of six songs he knew how to play. Then he made a

slot to insert money.

56

That evening Abe was so excited that he didn't have much of an

_____ for dinner. At 6:30, his dad helped him transport
16

everything to school. Once inside the gym, Abe set everything up. He taped

up a sign to _____ his service. It read, "Your Favorite Song
17

$1.00." Then Abe slid under the carton and stood holding his violin. He

waited for his first customer. "My friends can't say I didn't come," he thought.

"But boy, will I _____ them with this idea!"
18

Someone came over and put a dollar in the slot. "Play 'Yellow

Submarine' for me, Abe," Mike said.

Then Sydney came over. "Abe," she laughed, talking through the slot.

"May I have this dance?"

"How did you _____ it was me?" Abe said, after
19

shedding his disguise. "Only my feet were

showing."

"That was the trouble," said Sydney,

pointing to Abe's sneakers. "We'd

_____ your shoes anywhere!"
20

strike
surprise
style
science
violin
survive
realize
violet
notify
appetite
sigh
describe
deny
advertise
recognize
choir
silence
design
apply
assign

★ Challenge Yourself ★

Challenge Words

hypnotize
vibrant
imply
xylophone

Write the Challenge Word for each clue. Check a dictionary to see if you are right. Then use separate paper to write sentences showing that you understand the meaning of each Challenge Word.

21. You do it when you hint at an idea.

_____

22. The colors of tree leaves are this on a bright fall day. _____

23. This is something you might see and hear in an orchestra. _____

24. Some magicians do this to people as part of their acts. _____

Lesson 14 · Science Words

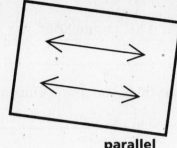

parallel

Spelling Word List

1. One-Syllable Words
   _____
   _____

2. Two-Syllable Words
   _____
   _____
   _____
   _____
   _____
   _____
   _____
   _____
   _____
   _____
   _____

3. Three-Syllable Words
   _____
   _____
   _____
   _____
   _____
   _____

4. Four-Syllable Word
   _____

merge
distort
appear
unusual
spiral
illusion
incorrect
background
clockwise
revolve
parallel
equal
foreground
profiles
slanting
square
concentrate
constantly
continue
object

Say and Listen

Say the spelling words. Listen for the number of syllables in each word.

Think and Sort

Look at the letters in each word. Think about the number of syllables in the word. Spell each word aloud.

1. Write the two spelling words that have one syllable.

2. Write the eleven spelling words that have two syllables. Draw lines between the syllables.

3. Write the six spelling words that have three syllables. Draw lines between the syllables.

4. Write the one spelling word that has four syllables. Draw lines between the syllables.

Use the steps on page 4 to study words that are hard for you.

Spelling Patterns

One Syllable	Two Syllable	Three Syllables	Four Syllables
m**e**rge	dis•tort	con•tin•ue	un•u•su•al

Name: _____ Date: _____

Spelling and Meaning

Antonyms Complete each sentence by writing the spelling word that is
an antonym of the underlined word.

1. The pasta tasted quite _____. <u>ordinary</u>

2. We watched the image _____ in the distance. <u>vanish</u>

3. Was your answer _____? <u>correct</u>

4. The lanes of this road _____ just outside of the city. <u>separate</u>

5. After people get off, the train will _____ its journey. <u>stop</u>

6. Did you cut the cake into _____ pieces? <u>unequal</u>

Clues Write the spelling word for each clue.

7. A circular staircase is this. _____

8. This word means "to do something nonstop." _____

9. The hands on a watch turn in this direction. _____

10. This geometric figure has four equal sides. _____

11. Magicians are known for creating this. _____

12. These lines are the same distance apart. _____

13. This word is the opposite of *background*. _____

14. If things rotate, they do this. _____

15. This is the scene behind the main object of a painting. _____

16. These are side views of faces. _____

17. This word means "something that can be seen." _____

18. If something is sloping, it is this. _____

19. You do this when you fix your attention on one thing. _____

Word Story One spelling
word comes from the Latin word *tortus*,
which meant "to twist and turn out
of shape." The spelling word means
"to turn or twist." It has the prefix *dis-*.
Write the word.

20. _____

Family Tree: *appear* Compare the
spellings, meanings, and pronunciations of the
appear words. Then add another *appear* word
to the tree.

appearance

21. _____

disappeared   disappear

appear

Lesson 14: Science Words
Core Skills Spelling 6, SV 9781419034107

Spelling in Context

Use each spelling word once to complete the selection.

Optical Illusions

Are your eyes fooled by pictures? Sometimes your brain makes an _____
                                                                              1
guess about what you see. For example, if you look at a _____ that has curved
                                                                         2
lines, they may look like they are turning _____ when they really aren't turning
                                                            3
at all. This is called an optical _____. Illusions _____ around
                                 4   5
the idea that you think you're seeing one thing, but really you are seeing something quite different.

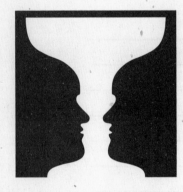

Does this picture show a vase, or does it show the

_____ of two people? The _____
          6   7

and the _____ move back and forth, depending upon
                 8

whether you focus on the profiles

or the vase.

The _____ lines here will
            9

_____ together in the distance. Their slant
     10

makes the _____ look wider at the top. To
                  11

get rid of the illusion, cover the lines around the square.

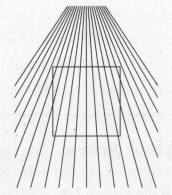

The many short lines in this design _____
                                                     12
the long lines so that the long ones do not _____
                                                            13
parallel. Lift the book and look at them at eye level, and they will

appear _____. They are really
               14

_____ distances apart.
       15

Stare _____ at the
16
black dot. As you _____, the
17
gray haze around it will appear to get smaller.

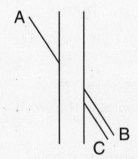

Does Line A _____ as Line B,
18
or does it become Line C? Use a ruler to find out.

What is strange or
_____ about this
19
_____?
20

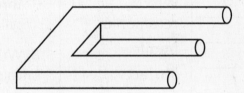

Word list:
- merge
- distort
- appear
- unusual
- spiral
- illusion
- incorrect
- background
- clockwise
- revolve
- parallel
- equal
- foreground
- profiles
- slanting
- square
- concentrate
- constantly
- continue
- object

★ Challenge Yourself ★

Challenge Words

geometric
symmetry
perpendicular
spherical

Use a dictionary to answer these questions. Then use separate paper to write sentences showing that you understand the meaning of each Challenge Word.

21. Are circles, squares, triangles, and rectangles examples
    of **geometric** figures? _____

22 Are the stripes on the highway **perpendicular** to each other? _____

23. Do a butterfly's wings show **symmetry**? _____

24. Is the shape of a shoe box **spherical**? _____

Name: _____   Date: _____

Lesson 15
Social Studies Words

skeletons

1. Two-Syllable Words
_____
_____
_____
_____
_____
_____

2. Three-Syllable Words
_____
_____
_____
_____
_____
_____
_____
_____
_____

3. Four-Syllable Words
_____
_____
_____
_____
_____

society
excavation
influence
nature
woven
resources
behavior
skeletons
culture
ceremonies
fragile
artifacts
scientists
identify
region
climate
primitive
environment
adapted
evidence

Say and Listen
Say each spelling word. Listen for the number of syllables.

Think and Sort
Look at the letters in each word. Think about the number of syllables in the word. Spell each word aloud.

1. Write the six spelling words that have two syllables. Draw lines between the syllables.

2. Write the nine spelling words that have three syllables. Draw lines between the syllables.

3. Write the five spelling words that have four syllables. Draw lines between the syllables.

Use the steps on page 4 to study words that are hard for you.

Spelling Patterns

Two Syllables	Three Syllables	Four Syllables
wo•ven	ev•i•dence	en•vi•ron•ment

Spelling and Meaning

Definitions Write the spelling word for each definition.

1. remnants of ancient civilizations _____
2. the world of living things and the outdoors _____
3. things used to make other things _____
4. the way in which people or animals act _____
5. people who work in any of the sciences _____
6. a part of the earth's surface _____
7. the power to cause a change _____
8. a community that lives and works together _____
9. original, earliest _____
10. the natural conditions of a place _____

Synonyms Complete each sentence by writing the spelling word that is a synonym for the underlined word.

11. We studied the _____ of the ancient Aztecs. customs
12. The _____ of several buffalo were uncovered near the river. bones
13. Europeans _____ to life in the New World. adjusted
14. Scientists found _____ of dinosaurs in fossils. proof
15. The ancient clay vase was very _____. delicate
16. The _____ uncovered an ancient Roman city. dig
17. Can you _____ the seven continents? name
18. Many Native American _____ involved dance. rituals
19. Cloth was _____ to create large mats. interlocked

Word Story One spelling word comes from the Greek word *klima*, which meant "slope of the earth." We use the spelling word as a name for the weather conditions within a region. Write the word.

20. _____

Family Tree: *identify* Compare the spellings, meanings, and pronunciations of the *identify* words. Then add another *identify* word to the tree.

unidentified
21.
identifiable   identifies
identify

Spelling in Context

Use each spelling word once to complete the selection.

The Pueblo

Many years ago, the western _____ 1 of the United States had a much

wetter _____ 2 than it has now. At that time groups of _____ 3

nomadic people walked among herds of grazing buffalo and wild horses, hunting the animals for

food. Scientists have collected a great deal of _____ 4 about the lives of these

hunters by digging in _____ 5 sites. They discovered points of spears in the

_____ 6 of the animals they found.

When the land became too dry for grasses to grow, the huge animals people needed for food

died. The people became hungry, so they changed the way they lived. They

_____ 7 to changes in their _____ 8 by becoming food

gatherers. They lived on wild plants, nuts, fruits, and berries.

Later the people discovered how to grow their own food from seeds. Instead of going from

place to place, they settled down. They grew corn, beans, and other vegetables. They began to

build homes around the fields and formed small villages. All of these villages made up a

_____ 9

of people working and

living together. It was

during this time that the

people became known as

the Pueblo, and the Pueblo

_____ 10

began.

Today _____(11) who study peoples of the ancient past are able to name and _____(12) each Pueblo village. They do this by studying the _____(13) the people left behind. These must be handled with a great deal of care because they are old and very

_____(14).

Studies show that the Pueblo made beautiful pottery as well as baskets and other _____(15) goods. They also held special

_____(16) at certain times of the year.

The Pueblo have always held firm beliefs about the land. The day-to-day

_____(17) of the Pueblo people is in harmony with

_____(18). They have always believed that humans should take care of the land and other natural _____(19). This belief

continues to _____(20) the way the Pueblo live today.

society
excavation
influence
nature
woven
resources
behavior
skeletons
culture
ceremonies
fragile
artifacts
scientists
identify
region
climate
primitive
environment
adapted
evidence

★ Challenge Yourself ★

Challenge Words

anthropologist
colonize
populate
archaeologist

Write the Challenge Word for each clue. Check a dictionary to see if you are right. Then use separate paper to write sentences showing that you understand the meaning of each Challenge Word.

21. People do this to an area when they live in it.

_____

22. To build a colony is to do this. _____

23. This is a scientist who studies human culture. _____

24. This is a scientist who studies the remains of past civilizations. _____

Lesson 16

Words with /ŏ/

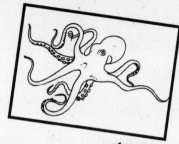

octopus

1. o Words

_____
_____
_____
_____
_____
_____
_____
_____
_____
_____
_____
_____
_____
_____
_____
_____
_____

2. a Word

_____

3. ow Word

_____

closet
ecology
comic
probably
astonish
knowledge
opposite
omelet
equality
molecule
impossible
forgotten
moccasins
proper
honor
octopus
tonsils
operate
honesty
demolish

Say and Listen

Say each spelling word. Listen for the /ŏ/ sound you hear in *closet*.

Think and Sort

Look at the letters in each word. Think about how /ŏ/ is spelled. Spell each word aloud.

How many spelling patterns for /ŏ/ do you see?

1. Write the eighteen spelling words that have the *o* pattern.

2. Write the one spelling word that has the *a* pattern.

3. Write the one spelling word that has the *ow* pattern.

Use the steps on page 4 to study words that are hard for you.

Spelling Patterns

o	**a**	**ow**
cl**o**set	equ**a**lity	kn**ow**ledge

Spelling and Meaning

Antonyms   Write the spelling word that is an antonym of each word below.

1. ignorance   _____
2. remembered   _____
3. disgrace   _____
4. improper   _____
5. possible   _____

Analogies   Write the spelling word that completes each analogy.

6. *Legality* is to *legal* as _____ is to *equal*.

7. *Lettuce* is to *salad* as *egg* is to _____.

8. *Cupboard* is to *dish* as _____ is to *coat*.

9. *Jungle* is to *tiger* as *ocean* is to _____.

10. *Lie* is to *dishonesty* as *truth* is to _____.

11. *Science* is to _____ as *mathematics* is to *geometry*.

12. *Mouth* is to *tongue* as *throat* is to _____.

13. *Alike* is to _____ as *early* is to *late*.

14. *Delicious* is to *flavorful* as *funny* is to _____.

15. *Build* is to *make* as _____ is to *wreck*.

16. *Huge* is to *mountain* as *tiny* is to _____.

17. *Surprise* is to _____ as *scare* is to *terrify*.

18. *Always* is to *sometimes* as *certainly* is to _____.

19. *Write* is to *author* as _____ is to *surgeon*.

Word Story   One spelling word comes from Native American tribes in North America and means "shoe." The Powhatans use the word *makasin* and the Ojibwas use the word *makisin*. Write the spelling word.

20. _____

Family Tree: *knowledge*

Knowledge is a form of *know*. Compare the spellings, meanings, and pronunciations of the *know* words. Then add another *know* word to the tree.

knowledge

21. _____

unknown   known

know

Spelling in Context

Use each spelling word once to complete the selection.

John Muir

"Do something for wildness and make the mountains glad," wrote John Muir, the man that people in the United States _____ 1 as the father of the national park system. Throughout his life, Muir encouraged the study of conservation and _____ 2 .

Muir was born in Scotland in 1838. At age 9, he sailed with his family to the _____ 3 side of the Atlantic Ocean—to the United States. From what we know, Muir was a healthy child with no serious health problems, not even sore _____ 4 .

Muir's father was a strict and _____ 5 man. He and his sons worked very hard on the family farm in Wisconsin. But whenever they had a chance, Muir and his brother roamed the countryside. The beauty and greatness of the land never failed to _____ 6 Muir.

Muir was an inventor and a carver. He made wooden clocks and a clever, even _____ 7 , invention that tipped him out of bed each morning! His _____ 8 of mechanical things got him a job in a carriage shop when he was 18. While he was there, he suffered a terrible eye injury. It was _____ 9 for Muir to see out of the injured eye. Doctors were unable to _____ 10 . The injury changed Muir's life. When his sight returned after a month, he promised to use his eyes to observe and describe nature.

In 1867 Muir began to walk from Indiana to the Gulf of Mexico. He walked through wildflowers in grassy valleys, _____ 11 wearing leather _____ 12 like those worn by some Native Americans. Eventually he moved to California, where he became fascinated with the Sierra Nevada mountain range.

In 1874 Muir began to write. He had not _____ his
13
promise to describe the natural world. Just as a chef uses different ingredients
to create an _____, Muir used words to write inspiring
14
articles about the importance of nature.

Meanwhile cattle and sheep were moved into many of the western
meadows and forests. Some people felt that the cattle and sheep would
_____ the natural landscape. Muir told the truth as he saw
15
it, and his _____ drew many followers. Muir and his friends
16
started the Sierra Club to protect the land.

Muir believed that because all things in nature are important, they
should be treated with _____. Today his work continues.
17
Scientists study animals large and small, from the _____ in
18
the ocean to the eagle in the sky. Even a _____ of water
19
receives attention.

People all over the world carry on the work of John Muir. What can you
do? Get your hiking boots out of the _____ and start
20
walking. Take time to enjoy the wonder and beauty of nature.

closet
ecology
comic
probably
astonish
knowledge
opposite
omelet
equality
molecule
impossible
forgotten
moccasins
proper
honor
octopus
tonsils
operate
honesty
demolish

★ Challenge Yourself ★

Challenge Words

allot
optimist
qualification
ferocity

What do you think each Challenge Word means? Check a
dictionary to see if you are right. Then use separate paper
to write sentences showing that you understand the
meaning of each Challenge Word.

21. Because we have an hour, we will **allot** ten minutes for
    each of the six speakers.
22. Because Yolanda is an **optimist**, she believes that everything will turn out
    well in the end.
23. My main **qualification** for the job of dog-sitter is that I love dogs.
24. The tiger growled with such **ferocity** that we all jumped back.

Lesson 17

Words with /ō/

telescope

Word List

1. o Words
_____
_____
_____

2. o-consonant-e Words
_____
_____
_____
_____
_____
_____
_____

3. oa Words
_____
_____
_____

4. ow Words
_____
_____
_____
_____

5. ough Word
_____

6. eau Words
_____
_____

noble
loan
throne
approach
grown
poetry
telescope
thrown
propose
lone
groan
microphone
plateau
suppose
solar
snowy
telephone
bureau
although
blown

Say and Listen

Say each spelling word. Listen for the /ō/ sound you hear in *noble*.

Think and Sort

Look at the letters in each word. Think about how /ō/ is spelled. Spell each word aloud.

How many spelling patterns for /ō/ do you see?

1. Write the three spelling words that have the *o* pattern.

2. Write the seven spelling words that have the *o-consonant-e* pattern.

3. Write the three spelling words that have the *oa* pattern.

4. Write the four spelling words that have the *ow* pattern.

5. Write the one spelling word that has the *ough* pattern.

6. Write the two spelling words that have the *eau* pattern.

Use the steps on page 4 to study words that are hard for you.

Spelling Patterns

o	o-consonant-e	oa
n**o**ble	l**o**n**e**	l**oa**n
ow	**ough**	**eau**
bl**ow**n	alth**ough**	bur**eau**

Spelling and Meaning

Making Connections Write the spelling word that completes each sentence and goes with the person.

1. The queen sat on her _____.

2. An officer at the bank gave the man a _____.

3. The writer created beautiful rhyming _____.

4. The singer used a wireless _____.

5. An astronomer uses a _____ to look at the stars.

Clues Write the spelling word for each clue.

6. People do this when they make a sad sound.   _____

7. Winter weather is this in some places.   _____

8. The sun creates this type of energy.   _____

9. People do this when they walk toward something.   _____

10. This piece of furniture has drawers.   _____

11. The wind has done this.   _____

12. This is another word for *guess*.   _____

13. This word is a synonym for *single*.   _____

14. A duke belongs to this kind of family.   _____

15. This is a word like *however*.   _____

16. If something has been tossed, it has been this.   _____

17. This word is a homophone of *groan*.   _____

18. If you make a suggestion, you do this.   _____

19. This is a high, flat area of land.   _____

Word Story The Greek word *tele* means "far away." The Greek word *phono* means "voice or sound." Write the spelling word that comes from these two Greek words and means "a device used to talk over a distance."

20. _____

Family Tree: *approach* Compare the spellings, meanings, and pronunciations of the *approach* words. Then add another *approach* word to the tree.

unapproachable

21.

approachable   approaches

approach

Spelling in Context

Use each spelling word once to complete the story.

The Coin Caper

Will and Claudia went to their local museum of natural history. They spent some time studying the lunar and _____ 1 eclipse exhibits. Then they went to a young people's workshop on the role of animals in art and _____ 2. Afterward they looked at a new exhibit showing animals that live in the high, flat _____ 3 regions of the world.

In the elevator Will read a poster announcing a sky show. The show featured a high-powered _____ 4. When he and Claudia got off the elevator, Claudia glanced out a window. It was a cold, _____ 5 day, and wind had _____ 6 the snow into deep drifts.

"I talked to Aunt Hattie a few weeks ago on the _____ 7," said Claudia, "and she said it was snowy in Maine, too. She's coming to visit soon."

"Speaking of Aunt Hattie," said Will, "there's the ancient coins display." As they began to _____ 8 the exhibit, they saw that it was blocked off. A woman was in there working alone. "Look!" Claudia cried out in surprise as she caught a glimpse of the _____ 9 woman. "What do you _____ 10 Aunt Hattie's doing here?"

Aunt Hattie walked over to Claudia. "My, how you've _____ 11 since this summer!" she said as she hugged her niece. She explained that she was reorganizing the entire coin collection, _____ 12 the museum had originally hired her to examine some old coins that had been discovered in an antique five-drawer _____ 13.

"Are you two still solving mysteries?" she asked. "I've got one for you. Look at this coin. It was found beneath the Pharaoh's _____ 14 in the Egyptian room."

"Oh, no!" said Will with a _____ 15. "I don't need any more mysteries!"

72

Claudia took the coin. "It was _____ 16 _____ there by a practical joker," she said. "It's worthless."

"It looks real," said Will, suddenly curious. "Isn't that a picture of some _____ 17 _____ person on one side?"

"Yes, but look at the other side," said Claudia. "It says 274 B.C. It can't be real. The terms B.C. and A.D. weren't used until 274 years later!"

"Right you are!" said Aunt Hattie. Just then someone in the main office spoke through a _____ 18 _____ to announce that the museum would close early because of the weather. "Good," said Aunt Hattie. "I _____ 19 _____ that we go have some lunch!"

"Great!" replied Claudia. "I'll call Mom and let her know." Then she laughed. "Aunt Hattie, could you _____ 20 _____ me a coin for the phone?"

noble
loan
throne
approach
grown
poetry
telescope
thrown
propose
lone
groan
microphone
plateau
suppose
solar
snowy
telephone
bureau
although
blown

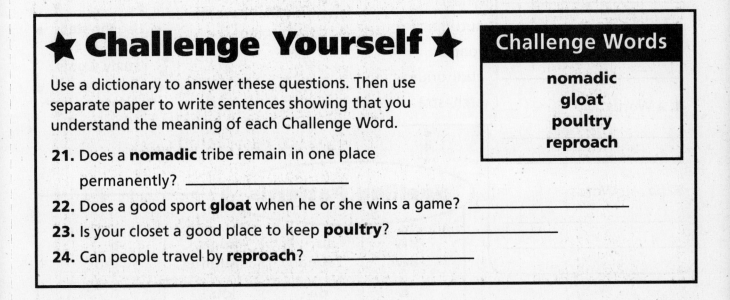

★ Challenge Yourself ★

Challenge Words

nomadic
gloat
poultry
reproach

Use a dictionary to answer these questions. Then use separate paper to write sentences showing that you understand the meaning of each Challenge Word.

21. Does a **nomadic** tribe remain in one place permanently? _____

22. Does a good sport **gloat** when he or she wins a game? _____

23. Is your closet a good place to keep **poultry**? _____

24. Can people travel by **reproach**? _____

Lesson 18 | Words with /ô/

audience

crawl
sword
ordinary
laundry
support
audience
awful
perform
formal
course
saucers
daughter
chalk
chorus
forward
wharf
autumn
coarse
auditorium
orchestra

1. *aw* Words

_____
_____

2. *au, augh* Words

_____
_____
_____
_____
_____
_____

3. *o* Words

_____
_____
_____
_____
_____
_____
_____
_____

4. *a* Words

_____
_____

5. *oa, ou* Words

_____
_____

Say and Listen

Say each spelling word. Listen for the /ô/ sound you hear in *crawl* and *sword*.

Think and Sort

Look at the letters in each word. Think about how /ô/ is spelled. Spell each word aloud.

How many spelling patterns for /ô/ do you see?

1. Write the two spelling words that have the *aw* pattern.

2. Write the six spelling words that have the *au* or *augh* pattern.

3. Write the eight spelling words that have the *o* pattern.

4. Write the two spelling words that have the *a* pattern.

5. Write the two spelling words that have the *oa* or *ou* pattern.

Use the steps on page 4 to study words that are hard for you.

Spelling Patterns

aw	au	augh	o
cr**aw**l	**lau**ndry	d**augh**ter	sw**o**rd

a	**oa**	**ou**	
wh**a**rf	c**oa**rse	c**ou**rse	

Spelling and Meaning

Classifying   Write the spelling word that belongs in each group.

1. cups   plates   _____
2. dock   pier   _____
3. rough   bristly   _____
4. run   walk   _____
5. shield   helmet   _____
6. eraser   blackboard   _____
7. sideways   backward   _____
8. horrible   terrible   _____
9. spring   summer   _____

Clues   Write the spelling word for each clue.

10. People use a compass to help them stay on this. _____
11. Musicians do this. _____
12. You need a washer and dryer to do this. _____
13. A tuxedo is an example of this type of clothing. _____
14. This contains many musicians and instruments. _____
15. This word is the opposite of *unusual*. _____
16. Walls do this to a roof. _____
17. This child is not a son. _____
18. A group of people sing together in this. _____
19. This is where singers may perform. _____

Word Story   One spelling word comes from the Latin word *audire*, which meant "to hear." The spelling word names people who listen to a performance. Write the word.

20. _____

Family Tree: *formal*   Compare the spellings, meanings, and pronunciations of the *formal* words. Then add another *formal* word to the tree.

informally

21. _____

formality   formalize

formal

Spelling in Context

Use each spelling word once to complete the story.

Peter Pan

Seven-year-old Ming was going to an afternoon performance of *Peter Pan*. It was a crisp, sunny _____ 1 _____ day, and Ming was excited as he rode on the bus with his father, a musician. Because they arrived early, Ming was allowed to go backstage.

Ming saw the harness that would _____ 2 _____ Peter Pan as he flew through the air. Mr. and Mrs. Darling's _____ 3 _____ evening clothes were being pressed in the wardrobe department. Ming also spied the large _____ 4 _____ that Peter Pan would use to battle the pirates, and he recognized the big lagoon where the *Jolly Roger*, Captain Hook's ship, was docked at the _____ 5 _____.

According to a notice written in white _____ 6 _____ on a blackboard, the cast and crew would be arriving soon to get ready to _____ 7 _____. Ming found his seat and watched his father and the other musicians in the _____ 8 _____ as they tuned their instruments. The _____ 9 _____ soon filled up with people. At two o'clock sharp, the performance began.

The play opened in the nursery of the Darling home. Mr. and Mrs. Darling said goodnight to their _____ 10 _____, Wendy, and their two sons, John and Michael. After Mr. and Mrs. Darling left and the children were asleep, Peter Pan flew in through the window. He was looking for his lost shadow. Tinkerbell, his tiny best friend, was behind him. Wendy woke up. She was amazed because Peter was no _____ 11 _____ boy—he could fly!

In Act Two of the play, John, Michael, and Wendy flew with Peter Pan to Never-Never Land. There they met pirates

and the gruff, _____ Captain Hook. Wendy became
12

mother to all the children there. She did their _____ and
13

washed their cups and _____.
14

When Tinkerbell saved Peter by drinking poison meant for him, she

began to fade away. Peter turned to the _____. He told
15

them that if people truly believed in Tinkerbell, she would get better. When

they leaned _____ in their seats, clapping as loudly as they
16

could, her light began to brighten.

In Act Three Captain Hook held all the children of Never–Never Land

captive on the *Jolly Roger*. They were saved when Tinkerbell led Peter to them.

Suddenly a big, _____-looking crocodile began to
17

_____ slowly up the plank after Captain Hook.
18

Ming had a wonderful time, and he hummed along when the

_____ sang, "I Won't Grow Up." Of
19

_____, he had trouble getting to sleep that night when he
20

thought about that crocodile. Wouldn't you if you were seven?

crawl
sword
ordinary
laundry
support
audience
awful
perform
formal
course
saucers
daughter
chalk
chorus
forward
wharf
autumn
coarse
auditorium
orchestra

★ Challenge Yourself ★

Challenge Words

notorious	brawn
audible	balk

Write the Challenge Word for each clue. Check a dictionary
to see if you are right. Then use separate paper to write
sentences showing that you understand the meaning of
each Challenge Word.

21. When people speak in a soft whisper, their voices are barely this. _____

22. A well-known criminal might be called this. _____

23. A horse might do this at the last minute instead of jumping over
a high fence. _____

24. A professional weightlifter is a good example of a person
who has this. _____

Lesson 18: Words with /ô/
Core Skills Spelling 6, SV 9781419034107

Lesson 19
Compound Words

thunderstorm

1. One-Word Compounds

_____
_____
_____
_____
_____
_____
_____
_____
_____
_____
_____
_____
_____
_____
_____
_____

2. Hyphenated Compounds

_____
_____
_____
_____

bathrobe
passport
weekday
brand-new
farewell
backpack
waterproof
proofread
chessboard
thunderstorm
flashlight
roommate
tablecloth
throughout
weekend
self-confidence
old-fashioned
eavesdrop
cross-country
applesauce

Say and Listen

Each of the spelling words is a compound word. Say each word. Listen for the two words that make up each compound word.

Think and Sort

The compound words in this lesson are written in two ways. Some are written as one word. Others are **hyphenated**—that is, they are written with a hyphen between them. Look at each spelling word. Think about how it is written. Spell each word aloud.

1. Write the sixteen compound words that are written as one word.

2. Write the four compound words that are hyphenated.

Use the steps on page 4 to study words that are hard for you.

Spelling Patterns

One-Word Compound	Hyphenated Compound
applesauce	old-fashioned

Core Skills Spelling 6, SV 9781419034107

Spelling and Meaning

Making Connections Complete each sentence by writing the spelling word that goes with the person.

1. A chess player needs chess pieces and a _____.

2. A spy must sometimes _____ to get information.

3. A waiter will replace a _____ if it is soiled.

4. A world traveler needs a _____ to go from country to country.

5. A mountain climber needs a _____ for carrying things.

Analogies Write the spelling word that completes each analogy.

6. *Wick* is to *candle* as *bulb* is to _____.

7. *Water* is to _____ as *fire* is to *fireproof*.

8. *Long* is to *short* as _____ is to *local*.

9. *Fear* is to *terror* as *self-assurance* is to _____.

10. *Work* is to *weekday* as *play* is to _____.

11. *Computer* is to *modern* as *typewriter* is to _____.

12. *Prior* is to *before* as _____ is to *during*.

13. *Author* is to *write* as *editor* is to _____.

14. *Strawberry* is to *jam* as *apple* is to _____.

15. *Saturday* is to *weekend* as *Thursday* is to _____.

16. *Blizzard* is to *snow* as _____ is to *rain*.

17. *Class* is to *classmate* as *room* is to _____.

18. *Hello* is to *welcome* as *good-bye* is to _____.

19. *Bathe* is to _____ as *swim* is to *swimsuit*.

Word Story One of the spelling words comes from *eavesdrip*, the area where rain drips under the eaves of a house. This area once provided a place for people to hide and listen to conversations occurring in the house. Write the spelling word.

20. _____

Family Tree: *backpack* *Back* is part of the word *backpack*. Compare the spellings, meanings, and pronunciations of the *back* words. Then add another *back* word to the tree.

backwards

21.

backpack   backs

back

Spelling in Context

Use each spelling word once to complete the selection.

Camping All Year Round!

It's a starry night, and you stare up at the stars from the comfort of your sleeping bag. Your campfire blazes merrily. You don't worry about rain or lightning from a _____ 1 because it's the middle of winter. Winter? Yes, that's right. Many people love the challenge of winter camping.

Camping in winter takes a lot of strength and hard work, especially if it's primitive camping, the kind with no cars or snowmobiles—only the snowshoes and _____ 2 skis that you bring. Winter camping also requires that you know the area and remember safety rules. Winter camping is demanding, but it can also be rewarding. Learning to survive in the great outdoors can help build your strength and _____ 3 .

Maybe sleeping outdoors in the wintertime is not for you. Some national parks have trailer camps. A trailer can be almost like home. Some people bring a television for entertainment. You can even eat dinner on a fine linen _____ 4 if you wish. If you bring a _____ 5 , you and your _____ 6 can play a game of chess. There's no need to bundle up during the cold mountain nights, either. If your trailer is heated, pajamas and a _____ 7 will keep you cozy at the end of the day.

Most people camp during the summer, and you can meet a lot of new friends then. Beginning on Friday night and continuing through the rest of the _____ 8 , families pack up and flock to trailer-park campgrounds. They come and go every weekend _____ 9 the summer. Sometimes people are so close together that it's easy for

someone to accidentally _____ on your conversations.
                            10
If you want more peace and quiet, try _____ camping.
                                          11
Fewer people camp during the week.

   Perhaps you think camping the _____ way in the
                                      12
summer is exciting, and you also like the idea of saying

_____ to modern devices for a day or two. Then put on
        13
your _____ hiking boots, fill a _____
           14   15
with supplies, and head for the mountains. Pack tents, raincoats, and other

_____ gear in case it rains. You may also want to carry
        16
bottled water with you, as well as crackers, cereal, and

_____ .
        17
   Whether you choose summer or winter camping, try writing about your

adventures. Although it's hard to edit and _____ your
                                               18
writing in the dim light of a _____ , your classmates will
                                    19
enjoy reading about your experiences. Whether you camp near your home,

across the state, or even in a country for which you need a

_____ , you'll have a lot of exciting things to share.
        20

| bathrobe |
| passport |
| weekday |
| brand-new |
| farewell |
| backpack |
| waterproof |
| proofread |
| chessboard |
| thunderstorm |
| flashlight |
| roommate |
| tablecloth |
| throughout |
| weekend |
| self-confidence |
| old-fashioned |
| eavesdrop |
| cross-country |
| applesauce |

★ Challenge Yourself ★

Challenge Words

lipstick
handbook
secondhand
roller coaster

Use a dictionary to answer these questions. Then use
separate paper to write sentences showing that you
understand the meaning of each Challenge Word.

21. Would you serve dinner guests **lipstick** as a dessert?

   _____

22. Would you shop for a brand-new pair of tennis shoes at
    a **secondhand** shop? _____

23. Would you look in a sports **handbook** to learn the rules for soccer? _____

24. If you like to go fast and you're not afraid of heights, would you like
    a ride on a **roller coaster**? _____

Lesson 20

Words Often Confused

desert

1. Different Pronunciations
_____
_____
_____
_____
_____
_____
_____
_____
_____
_____
_____
_____
_____
_____
_____

2. Same Pronunciations
_____
_____
_____
_____

breath
breathe
all ready
already
choose
chose
dairy
diary
lose
loose
quiet
quite
accept
except
weather
whether
desert
dessert
cloths
clothes

Say and Listen

Say each pair of spelling words. Listen to the pronunciation of each word in the pair.

Think and Sort

The pairs of spelling words in this lesson are often confused because they have similar spellings. The words in most pairs are pronounced differently and have different meanings. The words in some pairs are pronounced the same but have different meanings. Look at each pair of words.

Think about how each word is pronounced and spelled. Spell each word aloud.

1. Write the eight word pairs in which the words are pronounced differently.

2. Write the two word pairs in which the words are pronounced in the same way.

Use the steps on page 4 to study words that are hard for you.

Spelling Patterns

Different Pronunciations	Same Pronunciation
breath, breathe	weather, whether

Spelling and Meaning

Classifying Write the spelling word that belongs in each group.

1. outfits   costumes   _____
2. eat   sleep   _____
3. forest   tundra   _____
4. salad   soup   _____
5. before   formerly   _____
6. still   silent   _____
7. journal   log   _____
8. sports   news   _____

Definitions Write the spelling word for each definition. Use a dictionary if you need to.

9. to fail to win _____
10. pieces of material woven or knitted from fibers _____
11. the air drawn into and exhaled from the lungs _____
12. to select _____
13. not securely fastened _____
14. more than usual _____
15. to take what is offered _____
16. other than _____
17. no matter if _____
18. to be fully prepared to do something _____
19. selected _____

Word Story In Old English *dag* meant "dough," and *daege* meant "a kneader of bread." Later, *daege* became *deie* and came to mean "a woman who milked cows." The place she worked was called *deierie*. Write the spelling word that comes from *deierie*.

20. _____

Family Tree: *except* Compare the spellings, meanings, and pronunciations of the *except* words. Then add another *except* word to the tree.

exceptional

21. _____

exceptions   exception

except

Spelling in Context

Use each spelling word once to complete the story.

The Wind and the Sun

March 16

Today Mr. Perkins took us on a field trip to a _____. After we learned
                                                        1

how milk gets from the cow into the huge milk tanks there, we ate our lunch. We spread some

big cotton _____ on the grass and had a picnic. It was hot and sunny, so we
                    2

took off our coats. Then it clouded up and became windy and chilly, and we had to put our coats

on again. Mr. Perkins said this reminded him of the Aesop fable called "The Wind and the Sun."

I want to remember it, so I'm writing it here in my _____.
                                                              3

North Wind and Sun were both very proud. Each thought himself to be the stronger

influence on the _____, so they decided to have a contest. "Let's see who has
                          4

more effect on crops," Sun said. "The one who helps them grow more is the stronger."

"I know better than to _____ one of your challenges," replied Wind. "You
                                  5

would win that contest. Do you see that man on the road? He is wearing a heavy coat on top of

his other _____. There is no person around _____ him. Let
                  6   7

us see who can get the man to take off his coat."

"Very well," said Sun. "Now we will be able to see _____ or not you are
                                                                  8

really stronger than I."

"I _____ know I am stronger," said Wind.
          9

"We shall see," said Sun. "Go ahead and see what you can do. And remember, it was you

who _____
            10

the coat contest."

It was still and

_____.
        11

Wind took a deep

_____. First he began to _____ out
      12   **13**

gently on the man. Then Wind blew harder. Finally Wind let out tremendous

gusts. But the man only pulled his coat tighter around himself and bent his

head down low. Wind was displeased, but he expected Sun to fare no better.

"Go ahead when you're ready," he said graciously.

    "Oh, I am _____ ready right now," said Sun. He
                        14

began to shine gently but steadily on the man. The man stood tall and made

the coat _____ at the collar. Then the man unbuttoned the
               15

coat. The steady heat from the brightly shining Sun made the countryside as

hot as a _____. The man threw off his coat.
           16

    "I don't understand," complained Wind. "I seldom

_____ any contest that tests my strength."
      17

    "Well," said Sun, "perhaps you should _____ wisely
                                     18

when there is a choice. I have proven that one obtains better results from

gentleness than from force."

    After hearing the story, we had _____, and Mr.
                                  19

Perkins asked if we were _____ to go home. Someone
                        20

asked if we had a choice, and everyone laughed.

Word List
breath
breathe
all ready
already
choose
chose
dairy
diary
lose
loose
quiet
quite
accept
except
weather
whether
desert
dessert
cloths
clothes

★ Challenge Yourself ★

Challenge Words

density	**destiny**
moral	**morale**

What do you think each Challenge Word means? Check a dictionary to see if you are right. Then use separate paper to write sentences showing that you understand the meaning of each Challenge Word.

21. The **density** of the crowd made moving about the room very difficult.

22. The sun's **destiny** was to win the contest.

23. The **moral** of the fable is that gentleness can be more powerful than force.

24. The team was losing, but Coach Batista's positive speech at halftime helped to boost their **morale**.

Name: _____   **Date:** _____

Lesson 21

Words with /ou/

howl

1. *ou* Words
_____
_____
_____
_____
_____
_____
_____
_____
_____
_____
_____

2. *ow* Words
_____
_____
_____
_____
_____
_____
_____
_____

howl
crowded
prowl
blouse
doubt
couch
cloudy
eyebrow
mound
allowance
ouch
wound
surround
coward
growled
pronounce
proudly
scout
snowplow
thousand

Say and Listen
Say each spelling word. Listen for the /ou/ sound you hear in *howl*.

Think and Sort
Look at the letters in each word. Think about how /ou/ is spelled. Spell each word aloud.

How many spelling patterns for /ou/ do you see?

1. Write the twelve spelling words that have the *ou* pattern.

2. Write the eight spelling words that have the *ow* pattern.

Use the steps on page 4 to study words that are hard for you.

Spelling Patterns

ou	ow
m**ou**nd	h**ow**l

www.harcourtschoolsupply.com
© Harcourt Achieve Inc. All rights reserved.

86

Lesson 21: Words with /ou/
Core Skills Spelling 6, SV 9781419034107

Spelling and Meaning

Classifying Write the spelling word that belongs in each group.

1. bulldozer, steamroller, _____

2. wail, whine, _____

3. snarled, howled, _____

4. hundred, _____, million

5. _____, foggy, rainy

6. jammed, packed, _____

7. eyelash, eyelid, _____

8. speak, say, _____

9. salary, _____, payment

10. happily, _____, grandly

Rhymes Write the spelling word that completes each sentence and rhymes with the underlined word.

11. Howard was no _____, but he was afraid of heights.

12. There was no _____ that we took the wrong route.

13. Miguel cried, "_____" when he dropped the heavy mail pouch on his foot.

14. We found a _____ of stones in the middle of the field.

15. We watched the bear _____ for trout in the stream.

16. My stuffed mouse wears a little white _____.

17. The fox on the _____ looked for chickens and other fowl.

18. I'm a real grouch when I have to sleep on a lumpy old _____.

19. I _____ the yarn around my knitting needles.

Word Story One of the spelling words comes from the Latin word *superundare. Super* meant "over," and *undare* meant "to flow in waves." Write the spelling word.

20. _____

Family Tree: *doubt* Compare the spellings, meanings, and pronunciations of the *doubt* words. Then add another *doubt* word to the tree.

undoubtedly

21. _____

doubtless   doubter

doubt

Lesson 21: Words with /ou/
Core Skills Spelling 6, SV 9781419034107

Spelling in Context

Use each spelling word once to complete the selection.

Of Dogs and Snow: The Iditarod

After a snowstorm many people sit comfortably on a _____ 1 in their home and wait for a _____ 2 to clear the roads. Imagine traveling on a snowy winding trail where there are no snowplows. Go a step further and suppose that you are traveling not by car or train, but on a dog sled.

Before snowplows or even paved roads existed, dog teams in Alaska would _____ 3 out trails to get from one place to another. Some trails went straight across the wilderness. Others _____ 4 through mountains and forests. The trail that connected Anchorage to Nome was called the Iditarod Trail. *Iditarod* comes from a Native American word that means "the distant place." Here's how to _____ 5 it: ī•dĭt´•ə•rŏd.

In 1925 many people in Nome suffered from an illness called diphtheria. A team of dogs and people from Anchorage raced across snow and ice to take medicine to Nome. The trip took more than 127 hours. Today's Iditarod Sled Dog Race honors the memory of that famous trip.

The Iditarod has been called the last great race on Earth. Dogs led by "mushers," who train and care for the dogs, compete in this race, which is more than a _____ 6 miles long. Contestants from all walks of life confidently and _____ 7 sign up to face the bitter winds that can freeze an _____ 8 or a cheek on contact.

The dogs, usually Siberian huskies, have thick winter coats. They wear booties made of a material as thin as a silk _____ 9 but as warm as a down coat. Humans bundle up in windproof parkas.

This race takes special equipment. It also takes careful planning. It would be easy to pile up a _____₁₀ of supplies on a sled. But racers try to stay within a weight _____₁₁. The lighter the sled, the longer and faster the dogs run. A first aid kit is a must on this race. If you get a blister, you might just say, "_____₁₂." In the middle of the Iditarod, however, a blister on a dog or a musher is very serious. If left untreated, it can become infected.

The weather is brutally cold, no matter whether the days are bright and sunny or dark and _____₁₃. Teams often race late into the night. Swirling snow may _____₁₄ them, making it impossible to see. A distant _____₁₅ may indicate that a wild animal is on the _____₁₆. Imagine being alone in the dark wilderness when a wild animal howled or _____₁₇.

No one can _____₁₈ that the Iditarod race takes a strong mind and body. Although only one winner will emerge from the _____₁₉ field of contestants, no competitor, whether animal or human, can be called a _____₂₀. The men, women, and dogs that cross the finish line are true heroes.

howl
crowded
prowl
blouse
doubt
couch
cloudy
eyebrow
mound
allowance
ouch
wound
surround
coward
growled
pronounce
proudly
scout
snowplow
thousand

★ Challenge Yourself ★

Challenge Words

towering
drowsiness
scoundrel
bountiful

Use a dictionary to answer these questions. Then use separate paper to write sentences showing that you understand the meaning of each Challenge Word.

21. Could you see a professional basketball player **towering** over a young fan? _____

22. Does someone overcome by **drowsiness** want to sleep? _____

23. Should you admire a person who is a **scoundrel**? _____

24. Would a farmer be unhappy about a **bountiful** harvest? _____

Lesson 22
Words with /ûr/

squirrel

Spelling List

1. er Words
_____
_____
_____
_____
_____
_____
_____

2. ir Words
_____
_____

3. ur Words
_____
_____
_____
_____
_____
_____
_____
_____
_____

4. or Words
_____
_____

curly
refer
personal
worst
purchase
furniture
thirsty
merchant
worry
disturb
current
squirrel
emergency
curtains
observe
murmur
prefer
service
urgent
occurred

Say and Listen
Say each spelling word. Listen for the /ûr/ sound you hear in *curly*.

Think and Sort
Look at the letters in each word. Think about how /ûr/ is spelled. Spell each word aloud.

How many spelling patterns for /ûr/ do you see?

1. Write the seven spelling words that have the *er* pattern.

2. Write the two spelling words that have the *ir* pattern.

3. Write the nine spelling words that have the *ur* pattern.

4. Write the two spelling words that have the *or* pattern.

Use the steps on page 4 to study words that are hard for you.

Spelling Patterns

er	ir	ur	or
ref**er**	thi**ir**sty	c**ur**ly	wo**or**st

Name: _____   Date: _____

Spelling and Meaning

Synonyms   Write the spelling word that is a synonym for each word.

1. wavy _____
2. buy _____
3. important _____
4. happened _____
5. bother _____
6. mumble _____
7. fret _____
8. assistance _____
9. shopkeeper _____
10. watch _____

Clues   Write the spelling word for each clue.

11. This is what you do when you look at your notes when making a speech. _____
12. This word is the opposite of *best*. _____
13. These cover windows. _____
14. This is how people who need water feel. _____
15. This word means "up to date." _____
16. An ambulance is often needed for this. _____
17. This word describes a person's diary. _____
18. This word means "to like better." _____
19. A table and chairs are pieces of this. _____

Word Story   One spelling word comes from the Greek word *skia*, which meant "shadow" and *oura*, which meant "tail." The spelling word names an animal that curls its long tail over its head to shade itself. Write the word.

20. _____

Family Tree: *disturb*   Compare the spellings, meanings, and pronunciations of the *disturb* words. Then add another *disturb* word to the tree.

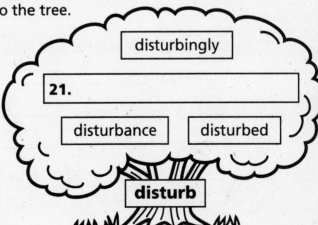

disturbingly

21. _____

disturbance   disturbed

disturb

Spelling in Context

Use each spelling word once to complete the story.

The Case of the Missing Pet

Will and Claudia stood in a pet store, where Claudia was about to

_____ a pair of chameleons from the
       1

_____, George Dunphy. "Hey, George," called his helper. "You've got a call.
       2

You'd better come quickly. It's Erica Dodson. She says it's _____."
                                                                         3

George picked up the phone. "Hello. . . . If it's a real _____, why not call
                                                                  4

the vet? . . . Oh, I see. Well, you do have a problem. But it just so happens that I can

_____ you to a pair of famous detectives. They give excellent
       5

_____, and they take a _____ interest in their cases. It's lucky
       6   7

that this _____ while they were here."
              8

In ten minutes Will and Claudia had reached Erica's house. She told them that her pet,

Ophelia, was loose in the house. "Don't _____," said Claudia calmly. "We'll find
                                                    9

Ophelia for you. By the way, what kind of pet is Ophelia?"

Before Erica could reply, the phone rang, and she left to answer it. Claudia went into the

kitchen and walked over to the cat bed near the stove. Will followed. "Ophelia can't be a cat,"

Claudia said in a low _____ to Will. "Nobody would get that upset over a cat
                               10

being loose!"

"The hair on this bed is reddish," said Will, examining it with a small magnifying glass.

"Maybe she's a red _____!" said Claudia. "Let's look around. But be
                            11

careful. She might get upset if we _____ her."
                                               12

Will looked under the living room _____. Then he looked behind the
                                               13

_____ on the windows. Claudia looked in the bathroom. Suddenly she
       14

screamed.

Core Skills Spelling 6, SV 9781419034107

"You found her!" yelled Erica, running into the bathroom. "Ophelia, you must have been _____ 15 and wanted a drink. Come on! Let's get you back into your cage!"

Erica thanked Will and Claudia for their help. The two headed back to the pet shop to purchase Claudia's chameleons. "Did you _____ 16 how calmly Erica handled Ophelia?" Claudia asked Will.

"Frankly," said Will with a shudder, "I _____ 17 a soft, _____ 18 -haired poodle any day to a snake. Is it a _____ 19 fad to own a python? I think snakes make the _____ 20 pets in the world."

"Me, too!" said Claudia as they walked into the pet store.

Word list: curly, refer, personal, worst, purchase, furniture, thirsty, merchant, worry, disturb, current, squirrel, emergency, curtains, observe, murmur, prefer, service, urgent, occurred

★ Challenge Yourself ★

Challenge Words
journalist   allergic
surgical   mirth

What do you think each Challenge Word means? Check a dictionary to see if you are right. Then use separate paper to write sentences showing that you understand each Challenge Word.

21. During his years as a **journalist**, he wrote many award-winning magazine and newspaper articles.
22. I must be **allergic** to grass, since I sneeze every time I mow the lawn.
23. The nurse brought the **surgical** instruments into the operating room.
24. The crowd's **mirth** showed in their smiles and laughter.

Lesson 23

Words with /ä/

carpenter

1. a Words

_____
_____
_____
_____
_____
_____
_____
_____
_____
_____
_____
_____
_____
_____
_____
_____
_____
_____
_____

2. ua Word

_____

carve
salami
barber
partner
guard
armor
marvelous
argument
apartment
marble
marvel
scarlet
arch
harbor
regard
carpenter
guitar
departure
harmony
harmonica

Say and Listen

Say each spelling word. Listen for the /ä/ sound you hear in *carve*.

Think and Sort

Look at the letters in each word. Think about how /ä/ is spelled. Spell each word aloud.

How many spelling patterns for /ä/ do you see?

1. Write the nineteen spelling words that have the *a* pattern.

2. Write the one spelling word that has the *ua* pattern.

Use the steps on page 4 to study words that are hard for you.

Spelling Patterns

a	ua
c**a**rve	g**ua**rd

Spelling and Meaning

Definitions Write the spelling word for each definition.

1. a curved structure over an open space _____
2. a fight with words; a disagreement _____
3. a small, rectangular wind instrument _____
4. something amazing _____
5. a person in business with another person _____
6. excellent _____
7. the act of going away _____
8. to look at closely _____
9. to watch over _____
10. someone who builds or works with wood _____
11. someone who cuts hair _____
12. to cut a piece of meat _____
13. a pleasing mix of musical sounds _____

Making Connections Complete each sentence by writing the spelling word that goes with the person.

14. A ship's captain docks her vessel in a _____.
15. Sculptors carve _____ statues.
16. A renter pays money to live in a house or an _____.
17. A sausage maker makes _____.
18. A folk singer plucks the strings on a _____.
19. A knight wears metal _____.

Word **Story** One spelling word comes from an ancient Persian word *säqirlat*, which meant "rich cotton dyed red." The spelling word means "a strong red color." Write the word.

20. _____

Family Tree: *harmony* Compare the spellings, meanings, and pronunciations of the *harmony* words. Then add another *harmony* word to the tree.

harmonizing

21. _____

harmonious   disharmony

harmony

Spelling in Context

Use each spelling word once to complete the story.

The House of Many Colors

Let me tell you about Sarah and Raymond.

Raymond is a _____ who builds tall
                        1

_____ houses. His
         2

_____ is Sarah. They had a really good
         3

reputation in town, but they argued a lot. Sarah and

Raymond used to have at least one

_____ every day. In fact, it got so bad
         4

once that someone said they should wear suits of

_____ to work. Their differences made
         5

it more and more difficult for them to work together.

    Sarah and Raymond are very different. You can tell

how different they are by the lunches they eat. Sarah always eats yogurt with fruit and nuts.

Raymond has something different every day. He has pizza with hot peppers and sausage or a

_____ sandwich with mustard and pickles.
         6

    Sarah likes to read and relax and feed the birds sunflower seeds after she eats lunch.

Raymond, on the other hand, likes to sing and strum his _____. He has one of
                                                              7

those funny-looking contraptions that holds a _____ around his neck.
                                                    8

Sometimes Frank, the _____ who protects the large building next door, comes
                            9

over. He harmonizes with the _____ who has a shop down the street.
                                    10

Raymond plays for the two of them. Their _____ is beautiful.
                                                11

    Remember I said that Sarah and Raymond used to argue a lot? Now things are different.

This is what happened. They were working on a house down near the water, just opposite the

_____. You have to go under a great big _____ to get there.
         12   13

Something _____ happened with this house. Sarah and
14
Raymond decided that instead of arguing, they would each do things the way
they wanted on this project.

The walls Raymond painted are cool colors like blue and green. But the
walls Sarah painted are hot orange, bright pink, yellow, and
_____. The doorways Raymond put in are average-sized
15
and plain. The doorways Sarah built are all different sizes and ornate. She had
someone _____ small figures into the wood. Raymond put
16
in plain wooden floors. The floors Sarah put in, however, have a checkered
pattern of _____ squares.
17

Some people might _____ this house as an eyesore. It
18
is certainly quite a _____ from the other houses in our
19
town. I like it. You should see it. It's a _____!
20

Word Box
carve
salami
barber
partner
guard
armor
marvelous
argument
apartment
marble
marvel
scarlet
arch
harbor
regard
carpenter
guitar
departure
harmony
harmonica

★ Challenge Yourself ★

Challenge Words

naive	**barter**
jargon	**marshal**

What do you think each Challenge Word means? Check a
dictionary to see if you are right. Then use separate paper
to write sentences showing that you understand each
Challenge Word.

21. The **naive** tourist did not know it was customary to tip the cab driver.

22. Farmers used to **barter** livestock, trading chickens for vegetables.

23. Please explain bytes and RAM to me in plain English, not computer **jargon**.

24. In the movie the town **marshal** arrested the outlaws.

Lesson 24 Words with Suffixes

honorable

1. -able Words

_____
_____
_____
_____
_____
_____
_____
_____
_____
_____
_____

2. -ible Words

_____
_____
_____
_____
_____
_____
_____

terrible
responsible
enjoyable
disagreeable
available
invisible
flammable
divisible
flexible
comfortable
breakable
usable
possible
remarkable
valuable
sensible
reasonable
lovable
honorable
probable

Say and Listen

Say each spelling word. Listen for the ending sounds.

Think and Sort

The endings -able and -ible are called suffixes. A **suffix** is a word part added to a base word that changes the base word's meaning. The suffixes -able and -ible mean "capable of" or "tending to be." Look at each spelling word. Think about what the word means and how it is spelled. Spell each word aloud.

1. Write the thirteen spelling words that end with -able.

2. Write the seven spelling words that end with -ible.

Use the steps on page 4 to study words that are hard for you.

Spelling Patterns

-able	-ible
us**able**	terr**ible**

Spelling and Meaning

Clues Write the spelling word that describes the person or object named in each clue.

1. an object that will shatter when dropped _____
2. someone who is sensible and fair _____
3. something that is fit for use _____
4. someone who does the right thing _____
5. a person who has good sense _____
6. something that can be divided _____
7. an activity that is fun _____
8. a person who is reliable and trustworthy _____
9. something that is likely to happen _____
10. something that can really happen _____
11. a person who is easily loved _____
12. something that is worthy of notice _____
13. a person who is never happy _____

Antonyms Complete each sentence by writing the spelling word that is an antonym of the underlined word.

14. Luís said the play was <u>wonderful</u>, but I said it was _____.
15. The thieves took some <u>worthless</u> items and some _____ ones.
16. This amazing new substance can be both <u>stiff</u> and _____.
17. Do you know if Sheila is _____ or <u>unavailable</u> for the meeting?
18. The flickering light was <u>visible</u>, and then _____.
19. The <u>fireproof</u> items survived the fire, but the _____ ones did not.

Word Story One spelling word comes from the Latin verb *confortare*, which meant "to strengthen." The spelling word includes the suffix *-able* and means "providing ease." Write the word.

20. _____

Family Tree: *agree* *Disagreeable* is a form of *agree*. Compare the spellings, meanings, and pronunciations of the *agree* words. Then add another *agree* word to the tree.

disagreeable

21. _____

disagree   agreed

agree

Spelling in Context

Use each spelling word once to complete the selection.

The Great Bargain Store

Luv-ums Shampoo People may like you now, but everyone will think you're quite

_____ 1 if you use GBS LUV-UMS SHAMPOO!

Pet Waterbeds We'll make any animal feel rested and

_____ 2 . See our own PET WATERBEDS.

Welsh for Americans It is

_____ 3 to learn Welsh in only 10 lessons. Buy *Welsh for Americans* at the book shop. Regular price $5.95 GBS price $6.00

Dimonrings Beautiful rings cheap! Our DIMONRING

looks just like a _____ 4 diamond. Yours for the

_____ 5 price of only $700.00

X. R. Sizer Keep your body slim

and _____ 6 ! Buy our X. R. SIZER now for $50.00 or pay only $10.00 a week for six weeks.

Brain Power Did you get

_____ 7 grades on your report card? Buy our BRAIN POWER cap and

experience a _____ 8 change in your thinking ability.

Color-Logs Try our COLOR-LOGS for your fireplace. These

_____ 9 logs are treated to give off bright colors as they burn, with no

_____ 10 odor.

Brainy Janey Are the numbers 16,830 and 16,803 evenly _____ 11 by 18? Find out in a flash with our BRAINY JANEY. This handy calculator makes doing math

_____ 12 .

Delicious! MR. PUMPKIN'S

SPICY BREAD is now

_____ at GBS.
          13
Made from flour, sugar, eggs, carrots,

water, and salt.

Invisi-Pills Just think of

what you could do if you were

_____! Buy
          14
our special Invisi-Pills and watch

yourself vanish into thin air. (We

are not _____
              15
for what you do after that.)

terrible
responsible
enjoyable
disagreeable
available
invisible
flammable
divisible
flexible
comfortable
breakable
usable
possible
remarkable
valuable
sensible
reasonable
lovable
honorable
probable

Marker Miracle Tired of all those dried-out markers that are no

longer _____? Trade them in for new ones. For every 5
              16
used ones you send in we'll send you 3 new GBS markers FREE! Include

$9.99 for shipping and handling.

Earth-Friendly Umbrella If rain is

_____, buy yourself or a friend our
          17
new Earth-Friendly Umbrella made from recycled

paper and cardboard. Make the _____
                                          18
choice—the Earth-friendly choice!

Great Glue Glass objects

are _____.
          19
When they break, you need

something to fix them. Use our

Great Glue! It will fix any break

you can make. (Not suggested

for use on glass objects.)

Finders Keepers Have you ever found

something and kept it, even if it wasn't yours? From now

on, do the _____ thing and turn it in
                20
to our Lost and Keep box. Just send in what you've

found and we'll make sure it gets to its rightful owner.

No details necessary! We prefer coins and bills.

Lesson 25 — Weather Words

thermometer

Spelling Word List

nimbus
humidity
temperature
flurries
wind-chill
forecast
long-range
atmosphere
pollution
Celsius
cumulus
velocity
cirrus
Fahrenheit
meteorologist
prediction
thermometer
thunderhead
precipitation
overcast

Sort Lists

1. Two-Syllable Words
_____
_____
_____
_____
_____
_____

2. Three-Syllable Words
_____
_____
_____
_____
_____
_____
_____
_____

3. Four-Syllable Words
_____
_____
_____
_____

4. Five-Syllable Word
_____

5. Six-Syllable Word
_____

Say and Listen

Say each spelling word. Listen for the syllables in the word.

Think and Sort

Look at the letters in each word. Think about how each syllable is spelled. Spell each word aloud.

1. Write the six spelling words that have two syllables. Underline the compound words.

2. Write the eight spelling words that have three syllables. Underline the compound words.

3. Write the four spelling words that have four syllables.

4. Write the one spelling word that has five syllables.

5. Write the one spelling word that has six syllables.

Use the steps on page 4 to study words that are hard for you.

Spelling Patterns

Two Syllables	Three Syllables	Four Syllables
nim•bus	at•mos•phere	ther•mom•e•ter

Five Syllables	Six Syllables
pre•cip•i•ta•tion	me•te•or•ol•o•gist

Spelling and Meaning

Compound Words Write the spelling word that is made from the two underlined words in each sentence.

1. The fisherman <u>cast</u> his line <u>over</u> the bridge. _____

2. Every <u>cast</u> member in the golfing movie cried, "<u>Fore!</u>" _____

3. The climbers felt the cold <u>chill</u> of the howling <u>wind</u>. _____

4. We rode our horses on the <u>range</u> for a <u>long</u> time. _____

5. Alicia turned her <u>head</u> when she heard the <u>thunder</u>. _____

Clues Write the spelling word for each clue.

6. light snow showers _____

7. a temperature scale on which water freezes at 0° _____

8. damage caused by chemicals and trash _____

9. made up of the gases surrounding the earth _____

10. what a thermometer measures _____

11. the amount of moisture in the air _____

12. someone who forecasts weather _____

13. a word that describes high, thin, wispy clouds _____

14. a temperature scale on which water freezes at 32° _____

15. what people make when they guess what will happen next _____

16. moisture that falls from the sky _____

17. a word that describes dark, low clouds _____

18. a word that describes big, white, fluffy clouds _____

19. the speed of the wind _____

Word Story   One spelling word comes from two Greek words: *thermos* and *metron*, which meant "hot" and "measure." The spelling word names a measurement instrument. Write the word.

20. _____

Family Tree: predict *Prediction* is a form of *predict*. Compare the spellings, meanings, and pronunciations of the *predict* words. Then add another *predict* word to the tree.

prediction

21. _____

predicts   predictable

predict

Spelling in Context

Use each spelling word once to complete the poem.

The Weather Forecaster

If you want to report the weather

Like Dr. Weatherright,

And make the weather _____
1

On the news show every night,

You must be a _____
2

Who studies the _____
3

To make an expert _____
4

On what the weather will be here.

You might say that the mercury in the

_____ will be rising,
5

So that a hot and torrid day

Will not be too surprising.

When you announce the

_____,
6

Be careful, if you please,

To give it in both _____
7

And _____ degrees!
8

On warm days the _____
9

Will make things hot and sticky.

If someone wants to paint a house,

It might be rather tricky.

Air _____ caused by fumes
10

From cars and factories assures

You'll have to tell the people,

"The air quality is poor."

When low gray _____ clouds
11

Make skies dark and _____,
12

You know there will be rain or snow

Before those clouds have passed.

Folks will wear their raincoats

If you warn of _____.
13

Or say that rain or snow

_____
14

Will hit part of the nation.

If you expect wild winter winds

Will make air seem more cold,

Be sure the _____ factor
                    15

Is a fact that folks are told.

If winter winds are going to blow

At high _____,
              16

Wrapped in scarves and earmuffs

Is how folks will want to be!

What kind of clouds are floating by—

Wispy tufts called _____?
                          17

If a _____ is on the way,
        18

You know a storm is near us.

But if skies are clear, or _____,
                                    19

Clouds are whipped cream in the blue,

Your _____, four-day
          20

Forecast will make a most popular you!

nimbus
humidity
temperature
flurries
wind-chill
forecast
long-range
atmosphere
pollution
Celsius
cumulus
velocity
cirrus
Fahrenheit
meteorologist
prediction
thermometer
thunderhead
precipitation
overcast

★ Challenge Yourself ★

Challenge Words

**frostbite
seasonal
evaporation
barometer**

Write the Challenge Word for each clue. Check a dictionary to see if you are right. Then use separate paper to write sentences showing that you understand the meaning of each Challenge Word.

21. This happens when the sun heats water on the ground and makes the water disappear into the air. _____

22. You could get this cold, painful condition if you walked barefoot a long way in the snow. _____

23. A meteorologist checks this to forecast the weather. _____

24. Temperatures that are normal for a certain time of the year are this. _____

Lesson 26

More Words with /ə/

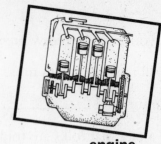

engine

Say and Listen

The weak vowel sound in unstressed syllables is called schwa and is written as /ə/. Say each spelling word. Listen for the /ə/ sound.

Think and Sort

Look at the letters in each word. Think about how /ə/ is spelled. Spell each word aloud.

How many spelling patterns for /ə/ do you see?

1. Write the five spelling words that have /ə/ spelled *a*.

2. Write the three spelling words that have /ə/ spelled *e*.

3. Write the four spelling words that have /ə/ spelled *i*.

4. Write the three spelling words that have /ə/ spelled *o*.

5. Write the five spelling words that have /ə/ spelled *u*.

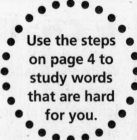

Use the steps on page 4 to study words that are hard for you.

Word List

pencil
triumph
history
pajamas
legend
injury
atlas
fortune
item
amount
balloon
circus
balcony
husband
focus
celebrate
cabinet
multiply
engine
purpose

1. /ə/ Words with *a*
_____
_____
_____
_____
_____

2. /ə/ Words with *e*
_____
_____
_____

3. /ə/ Words with *i*
_____
_____
_____
_____

4. /ə/ Words with *o*
_____
_____
_____

5. /ə/ Words with *u*
_____
_____
_____
_____
_____

Spelling Patterns

a	**e**	**i**	**o**	**u**
b**a**lloon	it**e**m	pen**ci**l	hist**o**ry	circ**u**s

Lesson 26: More Words with /ə/
Core Skills Spelling 6, SV 9781419034107

Spelling and Meaning

Clues Write the spelling word for each clue.

1. a place to sit in a theater _____

2. what a bruise or cut is _____

3. what people do at a birthday party _____

4. what sometimes floats high in the sky _____

5. chance or luck _____

6. what people do when they adjust a lens to get a clear image _____

7. the car part that runs _____

8. the opposite of *divide* _____

9. the story of the past _____

10. a book of maps _____

11. a synonym for *goal* _____

Classifying Write the spelling word that belongs in each group.

12. success, victory, _____

13. myth, tale, _____

14. thing, object, _____

15. closet, cupboard, _____

16. quantity, total, _____

17. pen, marker, _____

18. carnival, fair, _____

19. father, uncle, _____

Word Story One spelling word comes from the Persian words *pae*, which meant "leg," and *jamah*, which meant "clothing." *Paejamah* was an article of clothing that covered the lower part of the body. Write the spelling word that comes from *paejamah*.

20. _____

Family Tree: *fortune* Compare the spellings, meanings, and pronunciations of the *fortune* words. Then add another *fortune* word to the tree.

unfortunately

21. _____

misfortune   fortunate

fortune

| **Spelling in Context** | Use each spelling word once to complete the selection. |

Around the World in Twenty Days

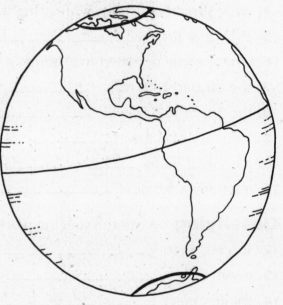

For ages, adventurers have found ways to travel all the way around the world. Find a map of the world in an _____ 1 and think about what it would be like to circle the earth.

Many people get the idea of traveling around the world from Phileas Fogg. Fogg is the hero of a novel written in 1873, *Around the World in Eighty Days.* Fogg circles the earth for a prize of $220,000, which was a small _____ 2 at the time the novel was written. The made-up story of Phileas Fogg, told years before flying around the world was actually possible, made Fogg almost a _____ 3. In 1999 a company offered a large _____ 4 of money—$1,000,000—to the first person or persons to make the journey by hot-air _____ 5. Two Europeans, Swiss doctor Bernard Piccard and British balloonist Brian Jones, were among many who accepted the challenge. Unlike the others, however, they made _____ 6 by winning the contest.

On March 1, 1999, Piccard and Jones started out in Switzerland. Jones's wife talked to her _____ 7 by satellite telephone and tracked the flight by radar.

The balloon used hot air heated by a gas _____ 8. Its cabin held bunks, desks, and a supply _____ 9 for such items as tools and instruments. One _____ 10 in the cabinet was a fax machine.

The men flew east toward Asia, never straying from their _____ 11—to fly nonstop all the way around the world in a hot-air balloon. As they traveled, Piccard and Jones

became the _____ of newspaper and television reports.
12

Students grabbed a pen or _____ and kept notes on the
13

balloon's progress. Children in _____ sat up late at night to
14

track the flight as it was shown on television and the Internet. The number of

onlookers began to _____. Soon it seemed as if the whole
15

world was watching, either on a television screen or through a telescope on a

back porch or _____.
16

As the men neared the goal, people began to _____.
17

Still, the mood was one of close competition, not of a three-ring

_____. By the end of their flight, Piccard and Jones had
18

become extremely tired but had escaped serious _____.
19

Twenty days after takeoff, Piccard and Jones landed in Egypt, which was well

beyond their starting point. Their balloon journey was a great

_____ of skill and courage.
20

pencil
triumph
history
pajamas
legend
injury
atlas
fortune
item
amount
balloon
circus
balcony
husband
focus
celebrate
cabinet
multiply
engine
purpose

★ Challenge Yourself ★

Challenge Words

luster
testimonial
exhilarating
inaccurate

What do you think each Challenge Word means? Check a dictionary to see if you are right. Then use separate paper to write sentences showing that you understand the meaning of each Challenge Word.

21. The pearls in her new necklace had a bright **luster**.

22. The ad had a **testimonial** by a woman who had used the soap for years.

23. A brisk walk in the crisp morning air can be **exhilarating**.

24. His measurements were **inaccurate**, so the boards were the wrong size.

Name: Date:

Lesson 27

Words with /ər/

soccer

1. /ər/ Words with *ar*

_____
_____
_____
_____

2. /ər/ Words with *er*

_____
_____
_____
_____
_____
_____
_____
_____
_____
_____
_____

3. /ər/ Words with *or*

_____
_____
_____
_____

cellar
fever
director
cheeseburger
modern
soccer
vinegar
hamburger
favorite
discover
customer
calendar
bother
similar
governor
computer
lunar
answer
effort
consumer

Say and Listen
Say each spelling word. Listen for the /ər/ sounds you hear in *cellar*.

Think and Sort
Look at the letters in each word. Think about how /ər/ is spelled. Spell each word aloud.

How many spelling patterns for /ər/ do you see?

1. Write the five spelling words that have /ər/ spelled *ar*.

2. Write the eleven spelling words that have /ər/ spelled *er*.

3. Write the four spelling words that have /ər/ spelled *or*.

Use the steps on page 4 to study words that are hard for you.

Spelling Patterns

ar	**er**	**or**
cell**ar**	answ**er**	eff**or**t

www.harcourtschoolsupply.com
© Harcourt Achieve Inc. All rights reserved.

110

Lesson 27: Words with /ər/
Core Skills Spelling 6, SV 9781419034107

Name: _____   Date: _____

Spelling and Meaning

Analogies   Write the spelling word that completes each analogy.

1. *Court* is to *basketball* as *field* is to _____.
2. *State* is to _____ as *country* is to *president*.
3. *Clock* is to *day* as _____ is to *year*.
4. *Up* is to *down* as *old-fashioned* is to _____.
5. *Chills* is to *cold* as _____ is to *hot*.
6. *Movie* is to _____ as *orchestra* is to *conductor*.
7. *Attic* is to *high* as _____ is to *low*.
8. *Moon* is to _____ as *sun* is to *solar*.
9. *Push* is to *shove* as _____ is to *annoy*.
10. *Clerk* is to _____ as *waiter* is to *diner*.

Definitions   Write the spelling word for each definition. Use a dictionary if you need to.

11. a piece of cooked ground beef served on a bun   _____
12. a hamburger with cheese   _____
13. an electronic machine used at home and at work   _____
14. someone who buys and uses goods or services   _____
15. something that is liked the most   _____
16. a reply to a question   _____
17. an attempt to do something   _____
18. almost the same as   _____
19. to find out   _____

Word Story   One of the spelling words comes from the Old French word *vinaigre*, which meant "sharp or sour wine." We use the spelling word to name wine that is fermented and used for things such as salad dressing. Write the spelling word.

20. _____

Family Tree: *director*   *Director* is a form of *direct*. Compare the spellings, meanings, and pronunciations of the *direct* words. Then add another *direct* word to the tree.

redirect

21.

directing   director

direct

Lesson 27: Words with /ər/
Core Skills Spelling 6, SV 9781419034107

Spelling in Context

Use each spelling word once to complete the selection.

May I Take Your Order, Please?

Running your own restaurant takes skill, a lot of hard work and _____ 1,

and a little bit of luck. Every year people open new restaurants. Many of the restaurants fail, but

some succeed.

Opening a restaurant begins with careful planning. First you must _____ 2

many questions. Where is the best place to locate? What days and times will your restaurant be

open? Will you serve breakfast, lunch, and dinner? If you're planning a neighborhood diner, you

may want to focus on breakfast and lunch and not _____ 3 with dinner.

Another decision you'll have to make is about the

dishes you will serve. Find out about your friends' and

neighbors' _____ 4 foods. Check out any

restaurant in the area that may be _____ 5

to yours. Then plan ways to stand out from the crowd. If

your restaurant will be a diner, you could decorate it to look

like one from the past. You could also make it look like a _____ 6 one of today.

Of course, you'll have to spend some time planning your menu. Try to give each

_____ 7 several dishes to choose from. If you start with a

_____ 8, you might want to add a slice of cheese to make a

_____ 9. Then add fries to the order. You might want to serve a garden salad with

oil and _____ 10 or another kind of salad dressing.

As a restaurant owner, you must be a smart shopper, or _____ 11. To help

keep track of how much money you spend on supplies, you'll want an up-to-date

_____ with good software. Search carefully to buy the
                12

freshest meats, fruits, and vegetables at the best prices. You might store supplies

in a basement or _____, which is usually cooler than a
                            13

room on the main floor. Observe local health codes. Keep everything in your

kitchen clean, since germs in food can cause stomach upset and

_____.
        14

    Now you can plan ways to get people to _____ you.
                                                        15

Do the local school students play _____ or hockey on
                                            16

Saturday mornings? Plan a special sports lunch menu that has Soccer Shakes

or Grilled Goalie Subs. If your restaurant is near the state capital, name a

sandwich or beverage after the _____. Look for an unusual
                                        17

event on the _____, such as a _____
                    18   19

eclipse. Invent a dessert to celebrate it, such as Disappearing Moon Cake.

    A restaurant owner is like the _____ of a movie. The
                                                20

kitchen and dining areas are movie sets. The actors are the cooks, servers, and

customers. The owner keeps everyone busy, happy—and eating!

Word List:
- cellar
- fever
- director
- cheeseburger
- modern
- soccer
- vinegar
- hamburger
- favorite
- discover
- customer
- calendar
- bother
- similar
- governor
- computer
- lunar
- answer
- effort
- consumer

★ Challenge Yourself ★

Challenge Words

indicator
calculator
hangar
rectangular

Use a dictionary to answer these questions. Then use separate paper to write sentences showing that you understand the meaning of each Challenge Word.

21. Does a fuel **indicator** show how much gas is left in the

    tank of an automobile? _____

22. Is a **calculator** helpful for solving a complicated math problem? _____

23. If you want to keep your best suit free of wrinkles, should you

    put it on a **hangar** in your closet? _____

24. Is the shape of the earth **rectangular**? _____

Name: _____   Date: _____

Lesson 28

More Words with /ə/

curious

1. /ə/ Words with *ou*

_____
_____
_____
_____
_____
_____
_____
_____
_____
_____
_____
_____
_____

2. /ə/ Words with *a*

_____
_____
_____
_____

3. /ə/ Words with *e*

_____
_____

4. /ə/ Word with *u*

_____

special
courageous
jealous
serious
spacious
generous
delicious
genius
social
mysterious
efficient
curious
commercial
various
nervous
ancient
tremendous
official
dangerous
conscious

Say and Listen

Say each spelling word. Listen for the /ə/ sound you hear in *special*.

Think and Sort

Look at the letters in each word. Think about how /ə/ is spelled. Spell each word aloud.

How many spelling patterns for /ə/ do you see?

1. Write the thirteen spelling words that have /ə/ spelled *ou*.

2. Write the four spelling words that have /ə/ spelled *a*.

3. Write the two spelling words that have /ə/ spelled *e*.

4. Write the one spelling word that has /ə/ spelled *u*.

Use the steps on page 4 to study words that are hard for you.

Spelling Patterns

ou	**a**	**e**	**u**
nerv**ou**s	speci**a**l	anci**e**nt	geni**u**s

Spelling and Meaning

Analogies Write the spelling word that completes each analogy.

1. *Nature* is to *natural* as *office* is to _____.

2. *Plain* is to *homely* as _____ is to *nosy*.

3. *Thoughtful* is to _____ as *jump* is to *leap*.

4. *Skyscraper* is to *modern* as *pyramid* is to _____.

5. *Courtesy* is to *courteous* as *mystery* is to _____.

6. *Unique* is to _____ as *happy* is to *joyful*.

7. *Brilliant* is to _____ as *brave* is to *hero*.

8. *Advertisement* is to *magazine* as _____ is to *television*.

9. *Tiny* is to *petite* as _____ is to *enormous*.

10. *Unproductive* is to _____ as *empty* is to *full*.

11. *Real* is to *reality* as _____ is to *society*.

Synonyms Complete each sentence by writing the spelling word that is a synonym for the underlined word.

12. Our ten-room apartment is very _____. roomy

13. Fighting a forest fire is a _____ thing to do. brave

14. Sometimes Theo was a bit _____ of his best friend. envious

15. I get _____ when I have to make a speech. worried

16. The students thought of _____ ways to solve the problem. different

17. The restaurant serves _____ food. tasty

18. Are you _____ of the fact that your shoelaces are untied? aware

19. Volunteer workers are _____ people. unselfish

Word Story Long ago the Latin word *dominiarium* meant "the risk of harm." The French, who spelled the word *dangier*, passed it on the English. Write the spelling word that comes from *dangier*.

20. _____

Family Tree: *social* Compare the spellings, meanings, and pronunciations of the *social* words. Then add another *social* word to the tree.

- socialize
- 21. _____
- socially
- antisocial
- social

Spelling in Context

Use each spelling word once to complete the letter.

Phoebe Zub Is Growing Dimmer Every Day

1543.25 Saturn Way

Sea of Tranquility, Moon

Nocte 21.5, 2222

Dear Jop Jupy,

On Nocte 1.3 I saw a TV _____ advertising a new spaceship designed by
1

some amazing _____. It has a _____ photography studio with lots
2   **3**

of room for cameras. The engine is very effective. In fact, it is so perfectly _____
4

that it can go to Pluto and back on 3 Kirgetons of fuel. The _____ government
5

report by Vice-Chairbeing Ock rated it Flut 4, a very high rating.

It sounded wonderful. I sent in an order and was able to get one of these

_____ ships right away. (Don't be _____ of my good fortune—
6   **7**

just wait.)

I had expected the ship to be big, but it was _____!
8

I stepped inside because I was _____ to see how it handled. There were two
9

buttons on the panel marked "Distant Future" and "_____ Past." As I pushed the
10

first button, I was _____ of a quivery, _____ feeling in my
11   **12**

stomach, but I ignored it.

I flew around for about 4 Hubs and decided to head home. But suddenly my spaceship stopped

moving. "This is a bad sign and could even be _____," I thought. I opened the
13

hatch and stuck out my foot, but I couldn't see a single thing. It was a very unusual feeling. It was

also very _____ to stumble over _____
                14   15
objects I couldn't see.

    Suddenly I heard some noise. Feeling _____ and bold,
                                              16
I moved toward it. It seemed to be space creatures having a party or other

_____ gathering. They were kind and
       17

_____ and shared some of their party cake with me. It
       18

tasted _____, even though it was invisible. Afterward they
          19

directed me home from their planet, Xrixner, and I arrived without further

incident.

    Now you may find this all very amusing. But something very

_____ has begun to happen. Since I got back, I find myself
       20

growing dimmer every day. I seem to be fading away. I fear I will soon be

invisible like the Xrixnerians. I'm sure it would be very convenient for

practical jokes. But I'm worried just the same. Please come see me soon, while

you still can!

                    Love,

                    Phoebe Zub

Word list:

- special
- courageous
- jealous
- serious
- spacious
- generous
- delicious
- genius
- social
- mysterious
- efficient
- curious
- commercial
- various
- nervous
- ancient
- tremendous
- official
- dangerous
- conscious

★ Challenge Yourself ★

Challenge Words

**albatross
crucial
anonymous
diligent**

Write the Challenge Word for each clue. Check a dictionary to see if you are right. Then use separate paper to write sentences showing that you understand the meaning of each Challenge Word.

21. A scientist would not want anything to go wrong at this point in an experiment. _____

22. This type of student pays careful attention, studies very hard, and does every assignment. _____

23. This bird might be seen flying over water. _____

24. If you received this kind of gift, you wouldn't know where to send a thank-you note. _____

www.harcourtschoolsupply.com
117
Lesson 28: More Words with /ə/
Core Skills Spelling 6, SV 9781419034107

Name: _____   Date: _____

Lesson 29
More Words with Suffixes

performance

Spelling Word List

1. **-ance Words**
_____
_____
_____
_____
_____

2. **-ence Words**
_____
_____
_____

3. **-ant Words**
_____
_____
_____
_____
_____

4. **-ent Words**
_____
_____
_____
_____
_____

5. **-ment Words**
_____
_____

attendance
assistant
incident
assignment
sentence
intelligent
performance
instrument
constant
different
experience
ignorance
apparent
vacant
distance
instant
difference
entrance
absent
distant

Say and Listen
Say each spelling word. Listen for the ending sounds.

Think and Sort
Each of the spelling words in this lesson contains a suffix. A **suffix** is a word part added to the end of a base word. A suffix changes the meaning of a base word.

Look at the letters in each word. Think about how the suffix is spelled. Spell each word aloud.

How many suffixes do you see?

1. Write the five spelling words with the -ance suffix.

2. Write the three spelling words with the -ence suffix.

3. Write the five spelling words with the -ant suffix.

4. Write the five spelling words with the -ent suffix.

5. Write the two spelling words with the -ment suffix.

Use the steps on page 4 to study words that are hard for you.

Spelling Patterns

-ance	-ence	-ant
attend**ance**	sent**ence**	inst**ant**

-ent	-ment	
abs**ent**	instru**ment**	

Spelling and Meaning

Classifying   Write the spelling word that belongs in each group.

1. door, gate, _____

2. smart, brilliant, _____

3. helper, aide, _____

4. clear, obvious, _____

5. word, phrase, _____

6. empty, unoccupied, _____

7. event, instance, _____

8. unusual, dissimilar, _____

What's the Answer?   Write the spelling word that answers each question.

9. What does an actor in a play give? _____

10. What do you have when you have lived through an event? _____

11. A clarinet is an example of what? _____

12. What is a lack of knowledge called? _____

13. When you aren't present, what are you? _____

14. What is the amount of space between two places? _____

15. What is a very short length of time? _____

16. The number of people who are present is called what? _____

17. What do you call the amount of being different? _____

18. Homework is an example of what? _____

19. What word is a synonym for *continuous*? _____

Word Story   One of the spelling words comes from the Latin word *stare*, which meant "to stand." The prefix *dis-* meant "apart" or "away." *Distare*, then, meant "to stand apart." Write the spelling word that comes from *distare* and now means "far away."

20. _____

Family Tree: *assignment*

Assignment is a form of *assign*. Compare the spellings, meanings, and pronunciations of the *assign* words. Then add another *assign* word to the tree.

assignment

21. _____

reassigned   assigned

assign

Spelling in Context

Use each spelling word once to complete the selection.

The Story of Fiber Optics

For centuries people dreamed of sending images over a very long _____.
 1
For many years, however, _____, or lack of knowledge, about how light works
 2
made this dream impossible. Then Alexander Graham Bell and his _____,
 3
Thomas A. Watson, invented an _____ called the telephone. It didn't transmit
 4
images, but it did transmit sounds through copper wires. The telephone made quick, almost

_____, communication possible. Bell's first telephone call consisted of a single
 5
_____: "Watson, come here."
 6

Bell was also working on a _____ device, one that could transmit images
 7
as well as sounds. There was one major problem, though. How could light be made to move

through wires?

During the 1840s, scientists showed that light could travel along streams of water. In the

1920s, two _____ scientists discovered that light could be sent through long,
 8
slender rods of glass. This single _____ led to other important events. In 1930
 9
Heinrich Lamm, a medical student, transmitted light through a bundle of thin glass rods, called

fibers, so that he could look inside a body.

The _____ of the early glass fibers was poor. Light leaked out of the glass.
 10
Something was missing, but what? Then in 1954 a Dutch scientist named Abraham van Heel

discovered what had been _____ from past fibers. He added a covering. It
 11
became instantly _____ that the covering helped to keep the light within the
 12
fibers. Yet even with the coverings, the light waves still bent and leaked. Even a little leakage could

mean the _____ between success and failure.
 13

In the 1960s an engineer named Charles Kao was very interested in fiber optics. He gave

himself the _____ of finding a way to lower the loss of light. It took many
 14

years, but he finally succeeded. He discovered that the glass used for the fibers had to be pure for the best results.

Scientists everywhere were gaining _____ in the new
15
field of fiber optics. They shared their findings at meetings. As word spread, the soaring _____ at these meetings left few if any
16
_____ seats. Soon large companies became involved. The
17
_____ of big business into the picture provided more
18
money for research.

Today fiber-optic cables lie under the oceans. These cables send a
_____ stream of information to near and
19
_____ parts of the world. The next time you use the
20
Internet, think of the fiber-optic cables that make it all possible.

attendance
assistant
incident
assignment
sentence
intelligent
performance
instrument
constant
different
experience
ignorance
apparent
vacant
distance
instant
difference
entrance
absent
distant

★ Challenge Yourself ★

Challenge Words

innocence
investment
pendant
acceptance

Write the Challenge Word for each clue. Check a dictionary to see if you are right. Then use separate paper to write sentences showing that you understand the meaning of each Challenge Word.

21. This word is the opposite of *guilt*. _____

22. This might hang around your neck. _____

23. This word is the opposite of *rejection*. _____

24. You make this when you buy stocks or bonds, hoping to make more money.
_____

Lesson 30

Words with -tion or -ture

station

1. -tion Words

_____
_____
_____
_____
_____
_____
_____
_____
_____
_____
_____
_____
_____

2. -ture Words

_____
_____
_____
_____
_____

collection
fixture
fraction
correction
attention
future
agriculture
feature
transportation
station
election
signature
information
direction
education
population
conversation
invention
lecture
selection

Say and Listen
Say the spelling words. Listen for the ending sounds.

Think and Sort
Each spelling word ends in *-tion* or *-ture*. Look at the letters in each word. Think about how each word is spelled. Spell each word aloud.

1. Write the fourteen spelling words that have *-tion*.

2. Write the six spelling words that have *-ture*.

Use the steps on page 4 to study words that are hard for you.

Spelling Patterns

-tion	-ture
frac**tion**	fea**ture**

Spelling and Meaning

Word Forms Complete each sentence by writing the spelling word that is a form of the underlined word.

1. The telephone is an exciting _____. <u>invent</u>
2. Buses are one form of _____. <u>transport</u>
3. A college _____ can be very useful. <u>educate</u>
4. Our candidate won after an exciting _____. <u>elect</u>
5. The city's _____ grew to more than a million. <u>populate</u>
6. My mother and I had a great _____. <u>converse</u>
7. I made the _____ in my report. <u>correct</u>

Definitions Write the spelling word for each definition. Use a dictionary if you need to.

8. the act of watching and listening _____
9. things brought together for a purpose _____
10. a prepared talk given on one or more topics _____
11. a part of something that stands out _____
12. the period of time that will come _____
13. something you put in place to stay _____
14. data and facts _____
15. guidance, assistance, or supervision _____
16. the business of farming _____
17. a person's handwritten name _____
18. a regular stopping place _____
19. a choice _____

Word Story One of the spelling words comes from the Latin word *fractionem*, which meant "a breaking, especially into pieces." The spelling word names a small piece that is part of a whole. Write the word.

20. _____

Family Tree: *invention* *Invention* is a form of *invent*. Compare the spellings, meanings, and pronunciations of the *invent* words. Then add another *invent* word to the tree.

invention

21.

reinvented   inventor

invent

Spelling in Context

Use each spelling word once to complete the selection.

Sojourner Truth

Sojourner Truth was born into slavery in New York State in 1797. At that time New York possessed a large slave

_____. New York slaves often worked in

1

the fields because farming and _____ were

2

still very important. In 1827 New York passed laws that freed

its slaves. At the age of thirty, Sojourner Truth became a free

woman. For several years she thought about the

_____ she wanted her life to take. Then in

3

1843 she decided what she would do in the _____.

4

She would speak out against slavery.

At first only a small _____ of the people working in the antislavery

5

movement knew about the former slave named Sojourner Truth. But she was a very good

speaker and soon became well known. Even though she had no formal schooling or

_____, she was able to read people. She drew upon what had happened in

6

her own life and gave firsthand _____ about slavery. Often she would sell a

7

_____ of songs that she had written. Her speeches became the main

8

_____ of antislavery gatherings.

9

As the movement for women's rights became stronger, Sojourner began to

_____ for that cause, too. Soon she was working toward the

10

_____ of wrongs against both African Americans and women. Sojourner, the

11

first name that she had chosen for herself, means "traveler." Sojourner Truth had indeed

become a traveler, going from place to place to call for equality and fair treatment of African

Americans and women.

After the _____ of Abraham Lincoln and the
12

beginning of the Civil War, Sojourner Truth turned her

_____ to the soldiers. Often she would appear at a railroad
13

_____ with a _____ of different kinds of
14   15

food and supplies to give the men.

After the war, Sojourner became a _____ in
16

Washington. She helped freed slaves to find homes and jobs. Before the

_____ of electric streetcars, the only form of public
17

_____ was streetcars pulled by horses. Sojourner worked to
18

integrate streetcars for all people. Because of her efforts, she was called to the

White House to talk to Abraham Lincoln. Sojourner traveled to Washington,

D.C., to meet with the President. She had a _____ with
19

Lincoln and left with his _____ on a note.
20

Sojourner Truth died at the age of 86. She did much during her life to

improve the treatment of African Americans and women.

Word list:
- collection
- fixture
- fraction
- correction
- attention
- future
- agriculture
- feature
- transportation
- station
- election
- signature
- information
- direction
- education
- population
- conversation
- invention
- lecture
- selection

★ Challenge Yourself ★

Challenge Words

participation
fracture
elation
caricature

Use a dictionary to answer these questions. Then use separate paper to write sentences showing that you understand the meaning of each Challenge Word.

21. Is your **participation** required if you are to be an active member of a basketball or baseball team? _____

22. Would a bone need to mend and heal if it had a **fracture**? _____

23. Would losing an important game cause you to feel a sense of **elation**?

_____

24. Is a **caricature** of the President of the United States likely to be the President's official portrait? _____

Answer Key

Page 6
1. salmon, attract, catalog, mammal, camera, balance, rapid, magnet, gravity, command, alphabet, graph, passed, accent, scramble, imagine, sandwich, paragraph, photograph
2. laughed

Page 7
1. balance
2. gravity
3. catalog
4. camera
5. magnet
6. graph
7. sandwich
8. paragraph
9. accent
10. salmon
11. mammal
12. passed
13. command
14. attract
15. scramble
16. photograph
17. rapid
18. laughed
19. imagine
20. alphabet
21. Answers will vary; a suggested answer is *photographing*.

Pages 8–9
1. photograph
2. paragraph
3. rapid
4. scramble
5. camera
6. catalog
7. salmon
8. sandwich
9. gravity
10. magnet
11. accent
12. laughed
13. balance
14. attract
15. mammal
16. graph
17. imagine
18. passed
19. alphabet
20. command
21–24. Definitions and sentences will vary.

Page 10
1. agent
2. trace, parade, escape, invade, misplace, safety, hesitate, congratulate
3. mayor, disobey
4. complain, stain, raincoat, remain, entertain, explain
5. neighborhood, straight, weighted

Page 11
1. safety
2. invade
3. disobey
4. straight
5. misplace
6. entertain
7. remain
8. hesitate
9. weighted
10. stain
11. escape
12. complain
13. neighborhood
14. raincoat
15. mayor
16. explain
17. trace
18. congratulate
19. parade
20. agent
21. Answers will vary; a suggested answer is *explains*.

Pages 12–13
1. parade
2. mayor
3. safety
4. disobey
5. neighborhood
6. explain
7. misplace
8. raincoat
9. hesitate
10. straight
11. agent
12. remain
13. trace
14. invade
15. entertain
16. escape
17. weighted
18. stain
19. complain
20. congratulate
21. yes
22. yes
23. no
24. yes
Sentences will vary.

Page 14
1. length, tennis, envelope, energy, echo, excellent, insects, restaurant, metric, separate, success
2. instead, pleasant, headache, breakfast, measure, treasure
3. guessed, guest
4. against

Page 15
1. insects
2. tennis
3. length
4. headache
5. guest
6. envelope
7. breakfast
8. excellent
9. treasure
10. guessed
11. separate

Page 16
12. instead
13. against
14. pleasant
15. energy
16. echo
17. metric
18. measure
19. success
20. restaurant
21. Answers will vary; a suggested answer is *separating*.

Pages 16–17
1. breakfast
2. envelope
3. pleasant
4. guest
5. against
6. tennis
7. restaurant
8. treasure
9. success
10. guessed
11. insects
12. instead
13. excellent
14. echo
15. length
16. energy
17. measure
18. metric
19. headache
20. separate
21. indelible
22. questionnaire
23. imperative
24. repel
Sentences will vary.

Page 18
1. darken, weaken, often, lessen, listen, quicken, strengthen, fasten, kitchen, soften
2. person, onion, prison, lemonade, seldom, lesson, ransom, custom
3. captain, mountains

Page 19
1. mountains
2. soften
3. darken
4. weaken
5. often
6. seldom
7. lessen
8. fasten
9. listen
10. strengthen
11. kitchen
12. ransom
13. prison
14. lesson
15. onion
16. person
17. custom
18. lemonade
19. quicken
20. captain
21. Answers will vary; a suggested answer is *Asian*.

Pages 20–21
1. captain
2. ransom
3. person
4. mountains
5. seldom
6. kitchen
7. often
8. custom
9. strengthen
10. quicken
11. fasten
12. lemonade
13. onion
14. lesson
15. listen
16. darken
17. soften
18. lessen
19. weaken
20. prison
21. no
22. no
23. yes
24. no
Sentences will vary.

Page 22
1. Caribbean Sea, North America, Indian Ocean, Atlantic Ocean, Pacific Ocean, Nile River, Rocky Mountains, Central America, Mediterranean Sea, Appalachian Mountains, Mississippi River, South America, Amazon River
2. Alps; Asia, Andes, Europe; Australia, Africa; Himalayas

Page 23
1. Alps
2. Nile River
3. Mississippi River
4. Europe
5. Rocky Mountains
6. Andes
7. Himalayas
8. Indian Ocean
9. Central America
10. Caribbean Sea
11. Mediterranean Sea
12. Asia
13. Amazon River
14. South America
15. Africa
16. Appalachian Mountains
17. North America
18. Australia
19. Atlantic Ocean
20. Pacific Ocean
21. Answers will vary; a suggested answer is *Asian*.

Pages 24–25
1. North America
2. Appalachian Mountains
3. Caribbean Sea
4. Central America
5. Rocky Mountains
6. Mississippi River
7. Indian Ocean
8. Africa
9. South America
10. Andes
11. Amazon River
12. Mediterranean Sea
13. Atlantic Ocean
14. Himalayas
15. Asia
16. Australia
17. Pacific Ocean
18. Alps
19. Europe
20. Nile River
21. Ganges River
22. Sahara
23. Antarctica
24. Bering Sea
Sentences will vary.

Page 26
1. meter, piano, memory, liter, library
2. breeze, brief, degrees, breathing, ceiling, succeed, piece, speaker, repeat, receive, increase
3. complete, scene
4. extremely
5. gasoline

Page 27
1. degrees
2. succeed
3. increase
4. repeat
5. brief
6. memory
7. complete
8. receive
9. extremely
10. speaker
11. breathing
12. piece
13. breeze
14. scene
15. liter
16. gasoline
17. meter
18. piano
19. library
20. ceiling
21. Answers will vary; a suggested answer is *breathed*.

Pages 28–29
1. degrees
2. receive
3. piece
4. increase
5. brief
6. piano
7. repeat
8. breeze
9. meter
10. extremely
11. succeed
12. scene
13. gasoline
14. liter
15. ceiling
16. breathing
17. complete
18. speaker
19. memory
20. library
21–24. Definitions and sentences will vary.

Page 30
1. thumb, struggle, umbrella, justice, difficult, crumb, discuss, plumber, result
2. government, tongue, compass, among
3. touch, trouble, double, enough, cousin, tough
4. flood

Page 31
1. compass
2. umbrella
3. government
4. enough
5. cousin
6. difficult
7. discuss
8. result
9. crumb
10. justice
11. tongue
12. among
13. flood
14. double
15. struggle
16. thumb
17. tough
18. trouble
19. touch
20. plumber
21. Answers will vary; a suggested answer is *crumbled*.

Pages 32–33
1. crumb
2. cousin
3. tongue
4. enough
5. government
6. justice
7. double
8. trouble
9. plumber
10. flood
11. discuss
12. umbrella
13. compass
14. difficult/tough
15. thumb
16. touch
17. struggle
18. among
19. result
20. tough/difficult
21. yes
22. yes
23. no
24. yes
Sentences will vary.

Page 34
1. student, human, smooth, humor, ruin, cruel
2. refuse, glue, renew, rude, threw, clue, pollute
3. coupon, canoe, improvement, through
4. nuisance, beautiful, juice

Page 35
1. canoe
2. juice
3. humor
4. human
5. pollute
6. nuisance
7. beautiful
8. through
9. improvement
10. coupon
11. renew
12. smooth
13. glue
14. threw
15. rude
16. refuse
17. cruel
18. clue
19. ruin
20. student
21. Answers will vary; a suggested answer is *humane*.

Pages 36–37
1. coupon
2. refuse
3. student
4. beautiful
5. through
6. improvement
7. ruin
8. pollute
9. glue
10. cruel
11. renew
12. rude
13. canoe
14. clue
15. smooth
16. threw
17. juice
18. nuisance
19. humor
20. human
21. boutique
22. tuition
23. neutral
24. intrude
Sentences will vary.

Page 38
1. canoes, holidays, voyages, pianos
2. tomatoes, mosquitoes, heroes, potatoes, echoes
3. knives, loaves, mysteries, memories, halves, industries, wolves, countries, bakeries, factories, libraries

Page 39
1. echoes
2. mysteries
3. heroes
4. countries
5. memories
6. loaves
7. industries
8. potatoes
9. halves
10. tomatoes
11. voyages
12. factories
13. pianos

Page 39 (cont.)
14. mosquitoes
15. canoes
16. bakeries
17. libraries
18. knives
19. wolves
20. holidays
21. Answers will vary; a suggested answer is *memorizing*.

Pages 40–41
1. countries
2. heroes
3. halves
4. factories
5. industries
6. mysteries
7. libraries
8. wolves
9. echoes
10. bakeries
11. loaves
12. potatoes
13. tomatoes
14. knives
15. canoes
16. mosquitoes
17. pianos
18. voyages
19. memories
20. holidays
21. yes
22. yes
23. yes
24. no
Sentences will vary.

Page 42
1. several, natural, hospital, carnival, general, principal, usually
2. nickel, novel, label, tunnel
3. wrestle, muscle, vegetable, grumble, castle, bicycle, example, whistle, principle

Page 43
1. carnival
2. example
3. label
4. nickel
5. grumble
6. general
7. several
8. usually
9. castle
10. vegetable
11. principal
12. natural
13. wrestle
14. novel
15. muscle
16. hospital
17. tunnel
18. bicycle
19. whistle
20. principle
21. Answers will vary; a suggested answer is *hospitalize*.

Pages 44–45
1. several
2. general
3. natural
4. grumble
5. novel
6. principal

7. muscle
8. example
9. tunnel
10. principle
11. nickel
12. usually
13. label
14. wrestle
15. castle
16. hospital
17. vegetable
18. whistle
19. carnival
20. bicycle
21–24. Definitions and sentences will vary.

Page 46
1. million, margarine, opinion, brilliant, definite, relative, scissors, liquid
2. rhythm, myth, system
3. select, experiment
4. business, electric, spinach, equipment, gymnastic, witness, detective

Page 47
1. scissors
2. million
3. liquid
4. spinach
5. margarine
6. select
7. relative
8. brilliant
9. rhythm
10. system
11. witness
12. myth
13. gymnastic
14. detective
15. business
16. experiment
17. opinion
18. definite
19. equipment
20. electric
21. Answers will vary; a suggested answer is *imagination*.

Page 48–49
1. definite
2. electric
3. myth
4. detective
5. system
6. brilliant
7. margarine
8. rhythm
9. business
10. gymnastic
11. equipment
12. relative
13. experiment
14. liquid
15. scissors
16. opinion
17. select
18. spinach
19. million
20. witness
21–24. Definitions and sentences will vary.

Page 50
1. luggage, cabbage, private, percentage, sausage, advantage, beverage, passage, message, storage, desperate, courage, average, chocolate, pirate, accurate, language, fortunate
2. immediate, image

Page 51
1. luggage
2. beverage
3. fortunate
4. accurate
5. private
6. average
7. message
8. language
9. passage
10. storage
11. cabbage
12. image
13. immediate
14. pirate
15. advantage
16. chocolate
17. sausage
18. desperate
19. percentage
20. courage
21. Answers will vary; a suggested answer is *imagination*.

Pages 52–53
1. advantage
2. message
3. courage
4. luggage
5. image
6. private
7. average
8. pirate
9. desperate
10. fortunate
11. immediate
12. passage
13. storage
14. percentage
15. language
16. accurate
17. cabbage
18. sausage
19. beverage
20. chocolate
21. no
22. no
23. yes
24. yes
Sentences will vary.

Page 54
1. strike, surprise, survive, realize, appetite, describe, advertise, recognize
2. notify, deny, apply
3. science, violin, violet, choir, silence, design, assign
4. sigh
5. style

Page 55
1. violin
2. appetite
3. science
4. notify
5. violet
6. realize
7. silence
8. design
9. assign
10. surprise
11. survive
12. recognize
13. apply
14. strike
15. describe
16. choir
17. style
18. sigh
19. deny
20. advertise
21. Answers will vary; a suggested answer is *surviving*.

Pages 56–57
1. strike
2. sigh
3. style
4. survive
5. science
6. deny
7. describe
8. silence
9. choir
10. assign
11. notify
12. violin
13. design
14. apply
15. violet
16. appetite
17. advertise
18. surprise
19. realize
20. recognize
21. imply
22. vibrant
23. xylophone
24. hypnotize
Sentences will vary.

Page 58
1. merge, square
2. dis/tort, ap/pear, spi/ral, back/ground, clock/wise, re/volve, e/qual, fore/ground, pro/files, slant/ing, ob/ject
3. il/lu/sion, in/cor/rect, par/al/lel, con/cen/trate, con/stant/ly, con/tin/ue
4. un/u/su/al

Page 59
1. unusual
2. appear
3. incorrect
4. merge
5. continue
6. equal
7. spiral
8. constantly
9. clockwise
10. square
11. illusion
12. parallel
13. foreground
14. revolve
15. background
16. profiles
17. object
18. slanting
19. concentrate
20. distort
21. Answers will vary; a suggested answer is *appears*.

Pages 60–61
1. incorrect
2. spiral
3. clockwise
4. illusion
5. revolve
6. profiles
7. foreground
8. background
9. slanting
10. merge
11. square
12. distort
13. appear
14. parallel
15. equal
16. constantly
17. concentrate
18. continue
19. unusual
20. object
21. yes
22. no
23. yes
24. no
Sentences will vary.

Page 62
1. na/ture, wo/ven, cul/ture, frag/ile, reg/ion, cli/mate
2. in/flu/ence, re/sourc/es, be/hav/ior, skel/e/tons, ar/ti/facts, sci/en/tists, prim/i/tive, a/dapt/ed, ev/i/dence
3. so/ci/e/ty, ex/ca/va/tion, cer/e/mo/nies, i/den/ti/fy, en/vi/ron/ment

Page 63
1. artifacts
2. nature
3. resources
4. behavior
5. scientists
6. region
7. influence
8. society
9. primitive
10. environment
11. culture
12. skeletons
13. adapted
14. evidence
15. fragile
16. excavation
17. identify
18. ceremonies
19. woven
20. climate
21. Answers will vary; a suggested answer is *identifying*.

Pages 64–65
1. region
2. climate
3. primitive
4. evidence
5. excavation
6. skeletons
7. adapted
8. environment
9. society
10. culture
11. scientists
12. identify
13. artifacts
14. fragile
15. woven
16. ceremonies
17. behavior
18. nature
19. resources
20. influence
21. populate
22. colonize
23. anthropologist
24. archaeologist
Sentences will vary.

Page 66
1. closet, ecology, comic, probably, astonish, opposite, omelet, molecule, impossible, forgotten, moccasins, proper, honor, octopus, tonsils, operate, honesty, demolish
2. equality
3. knowledge

Page 67
1. knowledge
2. forgotten
3. honor
4. proper
5. impossible
6. equality
7. omelet
8. closet
9. octopus
10. honesty
11. ecology
12. tonsils
13. opposite
14. comic
15. demolish
16. molecule
17. astonish
18. probably
19. operate
20. moccasins
21. Answers will vary; a suggested answer is *approached*.

Pages 68–69
1. honor
2. ecology
3. opposite
4. tonsils
5. proper
6. astonish
7. comic
8. knowledge
9. impossible
10. operate
11. often
12. moccasins
13. forgotten
14. omelet
15. demolish
16. honesty
17. equality
18. octopus
19. molecule
20. closet
21–24. Definitions and sentences will vary.

Page 70
1. noble, poetry, solar
2. throne, telescope, propose, lone, microphone, suppose, telephone
3. loan, approach, groan
4. grown, thrown, snowy, blown
5. although
6. plateau, bureau

Page 71
1. throne
2. loan
3. poetry
4. microphone
5. telescope
6. groan
7. snowy
8. solar
9. approach
10. bureau
11. blown
12. suppose
13. lone
14. noble
15. although
16. thrown
17. grown
18. propose
19. plateau
20. telephone
21. Answers will vary; a suggested answer is *informal*.

Pages 72–73
1. solar
2. poetry
3. plateau
4. telescope
5. snowy
6. blown
7. telephone
8. approach
9. lone
10. suppose
11. grown
12. although
13. bureau
14. throne
15. groan
16. thrown
17. noble
18. microphone
19. propose
20. loan
21. no
22. no
23. no
24. no
Sentences will vary.

Page 74
1. crawl, awful
2. laundry, audience, saucers, daughter, autumn, auditorium
3. sword, ordinary, support, perform, formal, chorus, forward, orchestra
4. chalk, wharf
5. course, coarse

Page 75
1. saucers
2. wharf
3. coarse
4. crawl
5. sword
6. chalk
7. forward
8. awful
9. autumn
10. course
11. perform
12. laundry
13. formal
14. orchestra
15. ordinary
16. support
17. daughter
18. chorus
19. auditorium
20. audience
21. Answers will vary; a suggested answer is *informal*.

Pages 76–77
1. autumn
2. support
3. formal
4. sword
5. wharf
6. chalk
7. perform
8. orchestra
9. auditorium
10. daughter
11. ordinary
12. coarse
13. laundry
14. saucers
15. audience
16. forward
17. awful
18. crawl
19. chorus
20. course
21. audible
22. notorious
23. balk
24. brawn
Sentences will vary.

Page 78
1. bathrobe, passport, weekday, farewell, backpack, waterproof, proofread, chessboard, thunderstorm, flashlight, roommate, tablecloth, throughout, weekend, eavesdrop, applesauce
2. brand-new, self-confidence, old-fashioned, cross-country

Page 79
1. chessboard
2. eavesdrop
3. tablecloth
4. passport
5. backpack
6. flashlight
7. waterproof
8. cross-country
9. self-confidence
10. weekend
11. old-fashioned
12. throughout
13. proofread
14. applesauce
15. weekday
16. thunderstorm
17. roommate
18. farewell
19. bathrobe
20. eavesdrop
21. Answers will vary; a suggested answer is *backed*.

Pages 80–81
1. thunderstorm
2. cross-country
3. self-confidence
4. tablecloth
5. chessboard
6. roommate
7. bathrobe
8. weekend
9. throughout
10. eavesdrop
11. weekday
12. old-fashioned
13. farewell
14. brand-new
15. backpack
16. waterproof
17. applesauce
18. proofread
19. flashlight
20. passport
21. no
22. no
23. yes
24. yes
Sentences will vary.

Page 82
1. breath, breathe, choose, chose, dairy, diary, lose, loose, quiet, quite, accept, except, desert, dessert, cloths, clothes
2. all ready, already, weather, whether

Page 83
1. clothes
2. breathe
3. desert
4. dessert
5. already
6. quiet
7. diary
8. weather
9. lose
10. cloths
11. breath
12. choose
13. loose
14. quite
15. accept
16. except
17. whether
18. all ready
19. chose
20. dairy
21. Answers will vary; a suggested answer is *exceptionally*.

Pages 84–85
1. dairy
2. cloths
3. diary
4. weather
5. accept
6. clothes

Core Skills Spelling 6, SV 9781419034107

7. except
8. whether
9. already
10. chose
11. quiet
12. breath
13. breathe
14. quite
15. loose
16. desert
17. lose
18. choose
19. dessert
20. all ready
21–24. Definitions and sentences will vary.

Page 86
1. blouse, doubt, couch, cloudy, mound, ouch, wound, surround, pronounce, proudly, scout, thousand
2. howl, crowded, prowl, eyebrow, allowance, coward, growled, snowplow

Page 87
1. snowplow
2. howl
3. growled
4. thousand
5. cloudy
6. crowded
7. eyebrow
8. pronounce
9. allowance
10. proudly
11. coward
12. doubt
13. Ouch
14. mound
15. scout
16. blouse
17. prowl
18. couch
19. wound
20. surround
21. Answers will vary; a suggested answer is *doubts*.

Pages 88–89
1. couch
2. snowplow
3. scout
4. wound
5. pronounce
6. thousand
7. proudly
8. eyebrow
9. blouse
10. mound
11. allowance
12. Ouch
13. cloudy
14. surround
15. howl
16. prowl
17. growled
18. doubt
19. crowded
20. coward
21. yes
22. yes
23. no
24. no
Sentences will vary.

Page 90
1. refer, per-

sonal, merchant, emergency, observe, prefer, service
2. thirsty, squirrel
3. curly, purchase, furniture, disturb, current, curtains, murmur, urgent, occurred
4. worst, worry

Page 91
1. curly
2. purchase
3. urgent
4. occurred
5. disturb
6. murmur
7. worry
8. service
9. merchant
10. observe
11. refer
12. worst
13. curtains
14. thirsty
15. current
16. emergency
17. personal
18. prefer
19. furniture
20. squirrel
21. Answers will vary; a suggested answer is *disturbing*.

Pages 92–93
1. purchase
2. merchant
3. urgent
4. emergency
5. refer
6. service
7. personal
8. occurred
9. worry
10. murmur
11. squirrel
12. disturb
13. furniture
14. curtains
15. thirsty
16. observe
17. prefer
18. curly
19. current
20. worst
21–24. Definitions and sentences will vary.

Page 94
1. carve, salami, barber, partner, armor, marvelous, argument, apartment, marble, marvel, scarlet, arch, harbor, regard, carpenter, guitar, departure, harmony, harmonica
2. guard

Page 95
1. arch
2. argument
3. harmonica
4. marvel
5. partner
6. marvelous
7. departure
8. regard
9. guard

10. carpenter
11. barber
12. carve
13. harmony
14. harbor
15. marble
16. apartment
17. salami
18. guitar
19. armor
20. scarlet
21. Answers will vary; a suggested answer is *harmonize*.

Pages 96–97
1. carpenter
2. apartment
3. partner
4. argument
5. armor
6. salami
7. guitar
8. harmonica
9. guard
10. barber
11. harmony
12. harbor
13. arch
14. marvelous
15. scarlet
16. carve
17. marble
18. regard
19. departure
20. marvel
21–24. Definitions and sentences will vary.

Page 98
1. enjoyable, disagreeable, available, flammable, comfortable, breakable, usable, remarkable, valuable, reasonable, lovable, honorable, probable
2. terrible, responsible, invisible, divisible, flexible, possible, sensible

Page 99
1. breakable
2. reasonable
3. usable
4. honorable
5. sensible
6. divisible
7. enjoyable
8. responsible
9. probable
10. possible
11. lovable
12. remarkable
13. disagreeable
14. terrible
15. valuable
16. flexible
17. available
18. invisible
19. flammable
20. comfortable
21. Answers will vary; a suggested answer is *agreeable*.

Pages 100–101
1. lovable
2. comfortable
3. possible
4. valuable
5. reasonable

6. flexible
7. terrible
8. remarkable
9. flammable
10. disagreeable
11. divisible
12. enjoyable
13. available
14. invisible
15. responsible
16. usable
17. probable
18. sensible
19. breakable
20. honorable

Page 102
1. nimbus, flurries, wind-chill, forecast, long-range, cirrus
2. atmosphere, pollution, Celsius, cumulus, Fahrenheit, prediction, thunderhead, overcast
3. humidity, temperature, velocity, thermometer
4. precipitation
5. meteorologist

Page 103
1. overcast
2. forecast
3. wind-chill
4. long-range
5. thunderhead
6. flurries
7. Celsius
8. pollution
9. atmosphere
10. temperature
11. humidity
12. meteorologist
13. cirrus
14. Fahrenheit
15. prediction
16. precipitation
17. nimbus
18. cumulus
19. velocity
20. thermometer
21. Answers will vary; a suggested answer is *predicted*.

Pages 104–105
1. forecast
2. meteorologist
3. atmosphere
4. prediction
5. Thermometer
6. temperature
7. Celsius
8. Fahrenheit
9. humidity
10. pollution
11. nimbus
12. overcast
13. precipitation
14. flurries
15. wind-chill
16. velocity
17. cirrus
18. thunderhead
19. cumulus

20. long-range
21. evaporation
22. frostbite
23. barometer
24. seasonal
Sentences will vary.

Page 106
1. pajamas, atlas, amount, balloon, husband
2. legend, item, celebrate
3. pencil, cabinet, multiply, engine
4. history, balcony, purpose
5. triumph, injury, fortune, circus, focus

Page 107
1. balcony
2. injury
3. celebrate
4. balloon
5. fortune
6. focus
7. engine
8. multiply
9. history
10. atlas
11. purpose
12. triumph
13. legend
14. item
15. cabinet
16. amount
17. pencil
18. circus
19. husband
20. pajamas
21. Answers will vary; a suggested answer is *unfortunate*.

Pages 108–109
1. atlas
2. fortune
3. legend
4. amount
5. balloon
6. history
7. husband
8. engine
9. cabinet
10. item
11. purpose
12. focus
13. pencil
14. pajamas
15. multiply
16. balcony
17. celebrate
18. circus
19. injury
20. triumph
21–24. Definitions and sentences will vary.

Page 110
1. cellar, vinegar, calendar, similar, lunar
2. fever, cheeseburger, modern, soccer, hamburger, discover, customer, computer, answer, consumer
3. director, favorite, governor, effort

Page 111
1. soccer
2. governor
3. calendar
4. modern
5. fever
6. director
7. cellar
8. lunar
9. bother
10. customer
11. hamburger
12. cheeseburger
13. computer
14. consumer
15. favorite
16. answer
17. effort
18. similar
19. discover
20. vinegar
21. Answers will vary; a suggested answer is *directions*.

Pages 112–113
1. effort
2. answer
3. bother
4. favorite
5. similar
6. modern
7. customer
8. hamburger
9. cheeseburger
10. vinegar
11. consumer
12. computer
13. cellar
14. fever
15. discover
16. soccer
17. governor
18. calendar
19. lunar
20. director
21. yes; 22. yes
23. no; 24. no
Sentences will vary.

Page 114
1. courageous, jealous, serious, spacious, generous, delicious, mysterious, curious, various, nervous, tremendous, dangerous, conscious
2. special, social, commercial, official
3. efficient, ancient
4. genius

Page 115
1. official
2. curious
3. serious
4. ancient
5. mysterious
6. special
7. genius
8. commercial
9. tremendous
10. efficient
11. social
12. spacious
13. courageous
14. jealous
15. nervous
16. various
17. delicious
18. conscious
19. generous

20. dangerous
21. Answers will vary; a suggested answer is *unsocial*.

Pages 116–117
1. commercial
2. genius
3. spacious
4. efficient
5. official
6. special
7. jealous
8. tremendous
9. curious
10. Ancient
11. conscious
12. nervous
13. dangerous
14. mysterious
15. various
16. courageous
17. social
18. generous
19. delicious
20. serious
21. crucial
22. diligent
23. albatross
24. anonymous
Sentences will vary.

Page 118
1. attendance, performance, ignorance, distance, entrance
2. sentence, experience, difference
3. assistant, constant, vacant, instant, distant
4. incident, intelligent, different, apparent, absent
5. assignment, instrument

Page 119
1. entrance
2. intelligent
3. assistant
4. apparent
5. sentence
6. vacant
7. incident
8. different
9. performance
10. experience
11. instrument
12. ignorance
13. absent
14. distance
15. instant
16. attendance
17. difference
18. assignment
19. constant
20. distant
21. Answers will vary; a suggested answer is *reassign*.

Pages 120–121
1. distance
2. ignorance
3. assistant
4. instrument
5. instant
6. sentence
7. different
8. intelligent
9. incident
10. performance
11. absent

12. apparent
13. difference
14. assignment
15. experience
16. attendance
17. vacant
18. entrance
19. constant
20. distant
21. innocence
22. pendant
23. acceptance
24. investment
Sentences will vary.

Page 122
1. collection, fraction, correction, attention, transportation, station, election, information, direction, education, population, conversation, invention, selection
2. fixture, future, agriculture, feature, signature, lecture

Page 123
1. invention
2. transportation
3. education
4. election
5. population
6. conversation
7. correction
8. attention
9. collection
10. lecture
11. feature
12. future
13. fixture
14. information
15. direction
16. agriculture
17. signature
18. station
19. selection
20. fraction
21. Answers will vary; a suggested answer is *invented*.

Pages 124–125
1. population
2. agriculture
3. direction
4. future
5. fraction
6. education
7. information
8. selection
9. feature
10. lecture
11. correction
12. election
13. attention
14. station
15. collection
16. fixture
17. invention
18. transportation
19. conversation
20. signature
21. yes
22. yes
23. no
24. no
Sentences will vary.

Core Skills Spelling 6, SV 9781419034107